OC 5 - '72

THE DAY
A TEAM DIED

Frank Taylor OBE

•

SOUVENIR PRESS

First published 1983 by Souvenir Press Ltd
43 Great Russell Street, London WC1B 3PD

Reissued in paperback 1995

Reprinted 1998
Reprinted 2003
Reprinted 2008

ISBN 9780285632622

Printed and bound in Malta by Progress Press Co. Ltd

Contents

To my wife
PEGGY
the sure shield; the strong right arm;
who never flinched even in
the Darkest Hours

Introduction

Not many people survive an air crash. I was one of the lucky ones who did. So were Sir Matt Busby and Bobby Charlton. Twenty-five years have now passed since Manchester United's young football team, returning in triumph from a European Cup tie in Belgrade, crashed at the end of the runway on Munich Riem airport, shortly after three o'clock on the snowy afternoon of Thursday, February 6th, 1958.

Those of us who survived need no calendar to remind us of that tragic day, the saddest ever in British sport. The memories are inscribed upon our minds until the day we die.

I have been asked many, many times why it was that, after two attempts to take off had failed, we all trooped back on to that airliner without any signs of panic or protest, for that third fatal take-off attempt.

The answer is very simple. We were all anxious to get home to Manchester, and as everyone must know, pilots do not take any risks because their lives are just as much in peril as their passengers.

So we went back on board, the engines roared into life, and in 54 seconds 23 people had been killed and the football legend of the Busby Babes was destroyed for ever.

Yet it was not only Manchester United who suffered in this tragedy. Newspapers suffered, with eight of the best sports writers I have ever known killed. They were my friends, and I learned so much from them that I have tried to carry on their style and tradition.

Some present-day colleagues may think that I overstate the brilliance of the Babes because I was emotionally involved. Of course they are entitled to hold that view, although personally I do not think English football has ever completely recovered from the Munich Air Crash.

Walter Winterbottom, who was manager of the England team

at that time, is still convinced England had the team to win the World Cup in 1958.

He has told me many times: 'You can never be completely sure of course, but I am in no doubt we had the players and the team spirit to win the World Cup in Sweden in 1958. We lost three key players in Roger Byrne, Duncan Edwards and Tommy Taylor in the Munich Air Disaster, and no international team can lose players of that calibre . . . It was just a tragedy for English football.'

Instead, the 1958 World Cup series brought glory to Brazil, and a 17-year-old wonder man named Pele. But I often wonder, would it have been a different story for Brazil, and especially for Pele, had he been playing against our superstar Duncan Edwards, who was himself only 21 but already an established international?

Years, they say, lend enchantment, but I am in no doubt that Duncan Edwards was the best English player since the end of World War II. It is a view shared by the former England captain Billy Wright. And I can think of no better way of describing the impact Edwards had on a game than Bobby Charlton's summing up:

'Compared to Duncan, the rest of us are just like pygmies. He had the lot . . .'

There is no doubt that the English game was never quite the same after Munich. The Babes were brash, brilliant, and attack-minded. Their obliteration coincided with a dramatic change in tactics, with almost every team playing a largely defensive game, so that young people now watching the game have never known anything different.

I hope young football fans of today may find something of interest in this book. I started to write it from my hospital bed in Munich, typing laboriously with one hand, because I wanted to leave some kind of lasting memorial to the Babes and my newspaper colleagues, and also because most of my life has been spent in front of a typewriter, and this was wonderful therapy.

Now, 25 years later, I have changed some parts of the original manuscript to bring the story up to date, although I saw no reason to change those parts of the narrative dealing with the air crash itself, because those words were written when every aspect and nuance of the tragedy was still fresh in my mind.

It is a story not exclusively about a football team, because this air crash went deeper than that. I wanted to pay tribute to the dedicated doctors, nurses and staff at three hospitals – the Rechts der Isar in Munich, the London Clinic, and Park Hospital Davyhulme. Without them, all would have been lost.

I doubt whether anybody could have been more squeamish than I was about having an operation. I hope those who feel the same way will gain in confidence from this story of how the medical teams managed to get us survivors back on our feet. We should marvel, and be forever grateful for those people who dedicate their lives to working with the sick and the maimed and the injured. Theirs is a calling which has uplifted mankind throughout the ages, with the flame of human kindness, in carrying out duties which cause the lesser among us to turn away from the often gruesome sights they see, and the deeds they are asked to perform in hospitals and casualty stations.

Those of us who were saved can never repay the debts we owe to so many people. This book is just one small way of saying thank you, to my wife, brothers, sisters and close family, but also to the doctors and nurses who not only helped me to get well again, but also to laugh again, just as we did in that Elizabethan airliner carrying the Manchester United party as she rode high in the skies over Central Europe on the afternoon of February 6th, 1958.

COME SIT WITH ME

1   The Flight to Munich

About 90 minutes after leaving Belgrade airport I was beginning to feel a trifle restless. It was not that I was nervous about the flight, but I was beginning to feel bored. There I was sitting alone, towards the front of the aeroplane, in a seat facing the rear. All my newspaper friends were sitting at the back, and I was feeling a little annoyed with myself for refusing to sit beside Frank Swift in the tail of the plane and insisting on moving to the front, simply because I could see there was more room up there in a group of seats facing the rear.

In Belgrade it had been a crisp cold morning: blue sky, a slight hint of sunshine and white snow on the ground. Not a lot. Just enough to make it look a Christmassy scene.

As we boarded our Elizabethan airliner, Frank Swift was already fastening his safety belt. When he saw me he waved and pointed to the empty place next to him.

'C'mon, Dad,' he shouted, 'I've kept this seat especially for you. Right back here in the tail which is the safest place.'

Swifty always said that, because in World War II so many tail gunners had been thrown clear and survived when their bombers crash-landed.

I shook my head: 'No thanks, Frank. There's a lot of space in those rearward facing seats up front,' I said.

'Be like that, Dad,' said Frank, laughing out loud. 'What's the matter, are you too good for the rest of us?'

I never did find out why Swifty always referred to me as 'Dad', although he was several years older than me. In fact, while I was still at school he had been one of my sporting heroes. I got to know him really well when he retired as England's and Manchester City's goalkeeper to write about soccer for the *News of the World*. I enjoyed his company, and the previous evening we had had a few convivial drinks together, so I was really looking forward to having a few more laughs with him on the flight home.

To this day, I don't know what caused me to refuse his kind offer to join him at the back of the aeroplane, except that I had once read that, in a terrible air crash, the only person to survive had been in a seat facing the rear of the plane.

I didn't want to explain all of this to Frank Swift, but just made my way forward and strapped myself in, hoping that one of the other sports writers would join me. In fact, they all had the same idea as Swifty, and I could see them laughing and joking, together. All eight of them.

So there I was, a talkative gregarious fellow, sitting alone and very bored with my own company, and without even a good book to read.

We were flying smoothly, chugging along at about 180 miles an hour, the twin propellers of the Elizabethan high-wing monoplane whirring endlessly, seemingly pulling us along towards West Germany.

Those were the days before jet travel, but there were two reasons why we were all pleased to be flying in an Elizabethan. One was that this particular aeroplane had been used to ferry Her Majesty the Queen, and we had been told that the Elizabethans had a good safety record. Up until that time, not one had crashed. I listened to the noise of the engines. There could be no doubt, the Elizabethan might be slow, but she looked like an aristocrat of the airways, and felt like one, as she droned on, nudging the clouds like a downy pillow.

I looked through the porthole to my right, where I could see the leading edge of the wing, as we seemed to be hanging, like a giant dragonfly against the canopy of the sky. Far below, the terrain looked rugged and fearsome, with mountains rearing out of the snowfield like a huge saw edge. The crevices in those mountains looked dark and evil, and the massive buttresses gave me the impression of being carved by a demoniacal stone mason in a fit of anger. One wondered how anyone could survive in such conditions, and I was glad we were flying so high.

The mountain range intrigued me. I couldn't decide whether they were the Dolomites, the Carnic Alps or the Karamanhe. In desperation, I turned to the neat folders and maps in the pocket at the rear of the seat in front of me. My sons Andrew and Alastair were then aged seven and six respectively. They were at an age where they took an interest in my travels, and I always liked to show them on maps where I had been, and the route the aircraft had taken. It was, I thought, a practical way of getting them interested in geography. After carefully studying the map, I decided the mountains below us must be the Carnic Alps, and then switched my attention to the other passengers. They were a happy group. Anybody who was anybody in British football was quite convinced that Matt Busby had brought to Old Trafford the most talented group of young footballers ever seen at any one club.

Busby's problem was not picking a team, but who to leave out. It was commonly acknowledged that, for the next decade at least, the Busby Babes – as they were known in the popular Press – were likely to dominate English Soccer. Busby still believes that this would have been the case. So do I, as I will explain later.

This year of 1958 was going to be Manchester United's Big Year. Busby thought so, and so too did his players. The previous season they had become the first English club to enter the European Cup, then dominated by Real Madrid. Incredibly those kids (for that is all they were) won the League Championship by a mile and reached the European Cup semi-final, before losing to Real Madrid, and they lost the Cup Final to Aston Villa only because their goalkeeper Ray Wood was cruelly injured.

Busby had put all that down to experience, and as I said, United were again chasing the honours. They were still in the FA Cup. The previous Saturday they had won an epic Football League clash with Arsenal at Highbury (still talked about nostalgically by true Arsenal fans) and in Belgrade they had drawn 3–3 with Red Star, which was enough to put them into the European Cup semi-final again.

No wonder the kids were happy. Things were just coming right for the team, although personally I was not quite convinced. Always, under Busby's managership, United played attacking football. They had good defenders, but the whole attitude of the team was directed to scoring goals. Thus, at Highbury, United had taken a 3–0 lead and then allowed Arsenal to get back into the game, to level the scores at 3–3. United scored a fourth goal; Arsenal equalised. Eventually United got their fifth goal and they won a nine goal match which sent the fans home delirious. That delirium included the Arsenal fans. This kind of result rarely happens in modern football. One goal away from home and the visiting team pulls nine players back to defend.

In the European Cup tie in Belgrade, two glorious Bobby Charlton goals, and another from Dennis Viollet, put United 3–0 by half-time. We in the Press Box thought the Babes were home and dry. Instead, they relaxed, and allowed Red Star to level the scores in the closing minutes.

I wanted to interview Matt Busby on this strange weakness. Were the defenders becoming too arrogant, or was the defence really weak? And if so, where?

I thought I could build up a nice follow-up story for the *News Chronicle* on that topic, but when I looked down the aeroplane to where Matt was sitting next to Bert Whalley, I could see he was dozing. Obviously there was no chance of having a chat with him on this leg of our journey home. I switched my attention to the other passengers. Across the gangway from where I was seated, burly Harry Gregg was curled up across three seats, having a cat nap. Behind Harry two men were conversing intently. They were Peter Howard, the *Daily Mail* photographer based in Manchester, and his colleague Ted Ellyard the telegraphist who had wired Peter's match photographs back to England. Peter Howard looked tired and drawn, but I was not surprised. We sports writers are often driven frantic, trying to telephone or telex a story back to our offices. With photographers – and more especially in those days – it was a terrible, nerve-jangling task.

Taking the photographs often in appalling conditions, getting them developed and printed and then sent back to England by wire, required very careful planning, plus an ability to converse in pidgin English and the smooth approach of a diplomat, to get through to foreign colleagues who did not then understand the speed with which Britain's national newspapers were produced. Sad to say, some of our newspapers now no longer have the speed and efficiency of production which was everywhere prevalent in 1958. Anyway, as I looked at the earnest face of Peter Howard I guessed he was suffering agonies of doubt about the transmission of his photographs.

Had they reproduced in good condition? Had the art desk

selected the best photographs? And even more important, had his shots arrived early enough to catch the first editions? When I thought about the problems they had faced, I was mildly surprised that Howard and Ellyard had not been reduced to gibbering fury.

My eyes wandered down the 'plane where, amidships, there was a lot of laughing and talking going on. That would be the card players. Johnny Berry, the perky little outside-right, was sitting there. So too was the team captain, Roger Byrne, and, although I couldn't see him, I could recognise the voice of Jackie Blanchflower. Usually, when travelling with an English soccer team, there is this hard core of card players who pass the time this way, rather than reading. Harry Gregg had intended joining that card school when we left Belgrade, but he wanted to use up his spare Yugoslav currency. After a lot of leg pulling, the other players decided the stakes would be in English money. Harry Gregg didn't agree; in any case he felt tired, so he moved forward to take his seat near the nose of the aeroplane. It was that snap decision which probably saved his life.

Farther back, in the tail of the machine, I could see all my particular friends: Henry Rose (*Daily Express*), Eric Thompson (*Daily Mail*), George Follows (*Daily Herald*) and the rest of the sports writers. They were obviously enjoying themselves, judging by the repeated outbursts of laughter.

I waved to them and shouted: 'There are plenty of seats up here.'

George Follows shouted back: 'What's the point? We are sitting comfortably here, and we would have to shift all our hand luggage.'

Just that one sentence. Had that reply not been in the negative, this would have been a very different and much happier story.

When I reflect now on those little incidents it all seems so strange, whereas at the time it seemed quite normal. Even the fact that I had gone forward to sit on my own; that was against my normal routine, because in those days I hated travelling on my own. I loved company, and as I have explained the only reason I took the decision I did, was because I had this theory about rearward facing seats being safer uppermost in my mind. There was also another lesser reason. The previous evening, I had suffered a queasy tummy through drinking red and white wine, then following that with beer. Frank Swift had also been slightly affected. On a previous flight to Prague, when I had had an upset stomach, I had sat in the tail of the aircraft, and had felt dreadful as we flew over the Alps, because it was so bumpy. As I looked towards the tail of the Elizabethan, my newspaper friends did not appear to be suffering any bumpiness, so I went down to join them, passing on the way Tom Curry, the United trainer. He was puffing away at his pipe, quite unconcernedly. To see him sitting like that, looking for all the world like a kindly middle-aged gent, you could hardly imagine him putting this group of brash, bouncy young footballers through their rigorous training routines. But he did. The players respected him for what he was: a good old pro. He needed his quick sense of humour to cope with the Old Trafford Crazy Gang: Tommy Taylor, David Pegg and Eddie Colman. These three, and some of the others, were always looking for a chance to pull a prank on Tom Curry.

I hesitated as I came abreast of Matt Busby and Bert Whalley. They were sitting together on the starboard side of the aircraft, with Bert, as always, ruddy-cheeked and brimming with vitality.

Matt looked as grey-faced and tired as when he had boarded the aircraft in Manchester for the outward journey. A few days before, he had slipped quietly into a Manchester hospital for an operation on some veins in his leg. Not a big operation perhaps, but one that sapped a man's energy. Instead of travelling with his team to Belgrade, Matt should have gone to the South of France, but, being the kind of man he is, he decided there was no way he was going to miss this important European Cup tie in Belgrade. Whatever happened he wanted to be with his 'Babes'. Matt was certainly paying for that decision now. The 2,000 mile round trip, from Manchester to Belgrade and back, was knocking the stuffing out of him. He was still dozing, so I didn't disturb him but carried on down the gangway to where the other sports writers were sitting.

'GARÇON!' It was my humorous colleague, Eric Thompson of the *Daily Mail*. 'Could you find a cigar for my friend Rose. . .?' Eric started laughing: 'My dear Taylor, you shouldn't look so much like a waiter. Never mind, I'll have a brandy. According to the note in my diary it is exactly 3 months 2 weeks 5 hours and 33 minutes since you last bought me a drink.'

'I will treat that last remark with contumely,' I said and, turning to Henry Rose, asked him: 'How are you feeling, Henry?'

'In myself quite all right,' he said without a smile. 'Apart from the usual murmur in my heart, a touch of blood pressure, an arthritic knee and a broken arm . . . but in myself I feel champion.'

Henry chortled at his own joke. He always liked to poke fun at those miserable people who go through life listing a monotonous monologue of imaginary ailments.

Behind Henry and Eric sat Don Davies, better known to *Guardian* readers as Old International. With him was Tom Jackson of the *Manchester Evening News*. They were just looking out at the scenery, while George Follows of the *Daily Herald* and Archie Ledbrooke of the *Daily Mirror* sat close by, deeply engrossed in a crossword.

Follows paused from this task: 'I may be mistaken Taylor,' he said. 'But I thought I heard one of the engines misfire a moment ago. I take it you have checked this aeroplane properly.' George always liked to poke fun at me, because he had been an officer in the Army during World War II, whereas I had been in the RAF.

A loud snore came from Alf Clarke of the *Manchester Evening Chronicle*, who was fast asleep with his mouth wide open: 'Alf must have been reading one of his own stories,' said George. 'It's the best cure for insomnia that I know.'

All the seats in the rear of the machine were occupied, so I had to stand chatting to my friends.

'You are a chump,' said Frank Swift. 'You wouldn't need to stand if you had taken the seat I offered you . . . By the way, have I ever told you about the Italian umbrella man?'

'Carry on,' I said. So Swifty launched into his tale of the English team playing in Italy. A game which England won 4–0.

'Believe me, it was daylight robbery,' Swifty told us. 'The Italians were practically camped in our half of the field, but I had one of those days when every time I stuck out my hand the ball hit it. Every time we broke away we scored, and naturally the Italian supporters weren't very pleased. One of them managed somehow to climb over the fence and get over the moat on to the pitch, carrying an umbrella. I don't know whether he was planning to hit the referee or one of our lads with it, but I came out of my goal and put my arms round his shoulders and managed to persuade him to get back off the field.

'At the banquet Sir Stanley Rous complimented me by saying I had acted with speed and diplomacy, and that, until then, he didn't know I could speak Italian.

'After the banquet, I got hold of Sir Stanley and told him the true story. I cannot speak any other language than English; all I did was to give this Eytie a big smile and say to him, "If you don't get off this field, mate, I'll wrap this brolly around your ruddy neck."

'The Italian couldn't speak English, but because I was smiling he thought I was paying him a compliment . . .'

That was a typical Swift escapade, and we were still laughing when the sign on the bulkhead was illuminated telling us to fasten our seat belts. I made my way back to my seat as the stewardess Margaret Bellis told us over the intercom:

'In a few minutes we shall be landing in Munich. Extinguish your cigarettes. No more smoking please, and fasten your safety belts. We will have time only for light refreshment in Munich, but we will be serving a proper meal after we take off for Manchester.'

I edged closer to the window to look down. So this was Munich. As with most Britons of my generation, I always associated Munich with Hitler and his Nazis, especially as it was the city that the British Prime Minister, Neville Chamberlain, had come to in 1938 to sign an agreement with Herr Hitler, in order to settle the Czech crisis. For some reason, it was a city which had a compelling attraction for me, so I felt a twinge of disappointment that this was only going to be a refuelling stop. I had read so much about Munich in my teen-age years that I wanted sometime to have a look at the famous art gallery, the elegant churches and the beer halls which were world famous, even before Hitler used them to recruit members for his Nazi Party.

I knew that Munich claimed to be a very beautiful city, but it looked as impersonal as any other city does, when you are suspended, so to speak, in space, before coming in to land. The Elizabethan, unlike the Viscount and other faster planes of that period, was circling slowly in ladylike fashion. A little ping in the ears indicated that we were losing height, and I could see that it was snowing quite heavily.

Dark lines etched like pencil lines across the pristine snow must be the runways, and that huddle of buildings the airport offices and restaurant.

Whoops! I felt the aeroplane plunge down quickly. She seemed to be losing height far too rapidly for my comfort. Down . . . down . . . down we went, with the high wing of the monoplane keeping us on an even keel. Now there were no bumps, no more unhappy feelings that my stomach was coming upwards into my throat. We had cut through the low lying clouds, although I realised it must be quite tricky for the pilots, Thain and Rayment, to keep the ship steady and bring her down safely in snowy conditions such as this.

I could see hedgerows whooshing past the portholes and realised yet again that it is only when landing or taking off that passengers are aware of the true speed of the aeroplane they are travelling in. We zoomed over the perimeter fence; one last downward thrust and we were skimming along the runway, with the wheels throwing back slush like a giant bow wave.

The snow had looked white and virginal from above, but here it had been churned into a dirty dark brown slush. I tensed and leaned even closer to an emergency exit, just in case the aircraft suddenly went into an uncontrollable broadside in these icy, slippery conditions. Easy with the brake now. Not too much, just enough to slow us down, in case we really did skid like a Grand Prix racing car.

At last we were just cruising down the runway, turning off towards the terminal buildings and the refuelling point.

I felt much happier now; we were safely down. The first part of the journey was over. It wouldn't take long to top up the airliner with petrol while we had a warm drink, and then we would be heading back home to our families in Manchester.

Yes, I was rather looking forward to seeing Peggy and the boys again.

2 Prelude to Disaster

As soon as the cabin door was opened the wind gusted in, bitingly cold, as though it had blown in from the frozen wastes of Siberia. Duncan Edwards led the rush down the airliner's steps, with the sleet lashing into the face like a razor.

Duncan looked even more massive than usual in his greatcoat, powerful arms pumping vigorously to get the circulation going:

'Get your snow shoes on, lads. Short studs are no use in this stuff,' he called over his shoulder, as he picked his way carefully over the squelchy treacherous surface of slush into the warmth of the airport lounge.

Munich airport now matches the best in Europe for its capacity, and the variety of its shops and offices. At that time it seemed just a huddle of buildings, but the lounge was warm. When I got there George Follows was already inside:

'If you fancy a cup of wet sawdust, try the coffee,' he said. 'The tea is a little better, but not quite up to NAAFI standards.'

I joined George, Henry, Eric and Archie in the annexe to the main lounge. Through the window, which ran the full length of the room, we had an uninterrupted view of the airfield. Tractors fussed around a cluster of aeroplanes, like dogs shepherding sheep into a pen. The main runways were like rivers or canals cut into an ocean of white, while all round the airport buildings dark lanes marked the paths of the aeroplanes as they came in to refuel. I could see the ground crew working on the Elizabethan and wondered whether, in these icy conditions, they were checking for ice on the wings as we did in Britain in wartime.

Out of the corner of my eye I noticed Eddie Colman making his way past the tables with several cups of tea in his hands. Even when he walked, Eddie appeared to be able to wriggle through the tightest corners. Here was a young player who was unique in style, beautifully balanced, very quick on his feet, with excellent ball control and an astonishing capability of being able to send his opponents completely the wrong way with a wiggle of his hips. It wasn't the graceful swerve for which Bobby Charlton is remembered, but rather, a quite extraordinary, skilful way of taking the ball right up to an opponent; then came the wiggle, and Eddie was off like a rabbit upfield, with the football still under control. Because of this, he had already been nicknamed 'Swivel Hips' or 'Snake Hips', and even 'the player with the Marilyn Monroe wiggle . . .'

All the nicknames caused Eddie acute embarrassment, and as he came towards us, Eric Thompson rose from his seat, placing both hands firmly on a table, as though to hold it down, saying to Eddie as he hurried past:

'Watch it Eddie . . . you nearly sent the table the wrong way with that body swerve . . .' Eddie grinned sheepishly and went on his way.

The door opened to admit one late straggler – Roger Byrne – and with him, a howling wintry blast of air. Byrne had a mania about fitness, and perhaps for that reason, generally scorned the luxury of a heavy overcoat, preferring to walk around briskly with no more than his blazer and flannels for protection. He always used to claim that deep breathing helped to keep him warm, and as he joined the party he gazed in mock astonishment at the howls of anguish at the cold wind he had brought in with him:

'What's the matter? Someone feeling the cold?'

Deep in an armchair, Duncan Edwards thundered: 'Shut that door, Rog,' as another player started to sing:

'Baby, it's cold outside.'

The Manchester United party were all male, apart from Mrs Miklos, the wife of the travel agent Bela Miklos. It was she who played the role of little mother, by going round every member of the party to enquire whether each had had a warm drink, and whether there was anything else we needed.

We were all a little anxious to be on our way home, although some of the players were having a last look round to buy presents for their families, particularly Johnny Berry, who kept the girl behind the toy counter busy winding up mechanical toys which he was considering buying for his children.

Tom Jackson of the *Manchester Evening News* seemed worried because he could not find his chief rival, Alf Clarke of the *Manchester Evening Chronicle*. Tom's routine rarely varied after a big game. He wrote late at night, and left his story under the telephone so that he could send it over first thing in the morning when he awakened. In this manner, he provided the vital early copy a large provincial evening newspaper needs. He was clearly worried in case Alf Clarke had picked up some exclusive piece of news which he didn't have. Which is why Tom was wandering around our group asking:

'Anyone seen Alf?'

'He's scooping you, Tom,' said George Follows, and then, seeing that Tom had taken him seriously added quickly: 'No, it's all right, there is no story.' Even as George was speaking, the call came over the tannoy:

'Will all passengers with the Manchester United party please board now . . .'

'Thank God for that,' said Henry Rose. 'We don't want any hold-ups. 'I've got to complete my postbag for the *Express* before going to the Press Ball tonight.'

Tom Curry stood quietly by the door, counting the number of players to make sure no one was left behind. We stood together in a group outside the lounge for a second check on the number of passengers, before squelching across the tarmac to where the Elizabethan was waiting. I paused for a moment as I entered the aeroplane, to see my Press colleagues fastening themselves in.

'I'll come back and join you as soon as we are airborne,' I said, then pushed my way through the crowded gangway to my own seat and fastened myself in. The engines were started, and quite soon, with the propellers whirring us along, we made our way to the take-off point. Already the cards were being shuffled in the centre of the 'plane as the stewardesses checked all cigarettes had been extinguished, and that we were all safely strapped in. The engines were revved up, first the port, then the starboard, as the pilots made their routine checks before take off.

Finally Thain and Rayment were satisfied, and the Elizabethan started to roll down the runway, gathering speed all the way. The time in Munich was just 14.30 hours and 40 seconds.

The sound of the engines rose from a gentle purr to a full-throated roar. Faster . . . faster . . . faster she whipped along. I looked out of my window to see the port wheel retract; then I would know we were airborne. Instead there was that same bow wave of slush and snow thrown back, just as it had when we landed. It was quite a shock not to see the port wheel slide smoothly upwards into the nacelle. Whoops! There was a sudden judder of the plane as the brakes were applied, and it lost speed. A little brake at first, then a little more as the engines lost their powerful roar.

From behind there came a clatter and I turned in time to see the steward, Tommy Cable, pitch into a seat behind Peter Howard. He appeared to be fastening his safety-belt.

'What are you doing that for, Tom?' I said. 'You'll give us heart failure. Anyone would think that something had gone wrong with the works.' I had met Cable before on these football trips, a cheery efficient type, very keen on sport. The usual stiff formalities between crew and passengers were often waived on such goodwill trips; that's why I called him by his Christian name.

He grinned. 'I got stranded up here on take-off when I should have been in the tail.' Whether Cable fell into that seat with the sudden braking, or whether he had dropped there of his own accord, I never did find out.

There was no discernible panic among the passengers but there were a lot of frowns and puzzled looks as the questions were fired man to man.

'What's the hold-up? Engines misfiring?'

'Didn't we reach take-off speed in time?'

'Has an engine suddenly cut?'

From the tail of the machine I could hear Archie Ledbrooke advancing his theory: 'Perhaps the water or slush has been thrown back into the electrical system and caused a short circuit.'

But no. Surely the electrical system was OK, for the lights were still on.

We had stopped halfway down the runway, just forty seconds after we had roared away from the take-off point.

It was now 14.31 hours and 20 seconds precisely.

In the cockpit the crew were busy explaining to the control tower that this take-off had been abandoned, and could they now have permission to back-track and try again? We, of course, could not know they had abandoned the attempt through a fluctuation of the boost pressures.

Boost pressure is the pressure in the engine manifold.

If it soars off the clock on take-off there is something radically wrong, and it could possibly lead to an engine seizure in mid air. This is what had been happening in the cockpit.

Captain Rayment, the co-pilot, was at the controls as the plane commander, Captain Thain, monitored the gauges and dials. Rayment called: 'Full power.' Thain replied: 'Temperatures and pressures OK. Warning lights out.' At this point he noticed an uneven note from the engines with the needles on the boost indicators fluctuating. Captain Rayment throttled back and braked, Captain Thain helping to hold the control column forward. Then they asked for permission to make a second run.

The pilots had now taxied the machine back to take-off and we were in position ready to go.

It was now 14.34 hours and 40 seconds.

Captain Rayment opened the throttles to twenty-eight inches of boost and then pushed the levers forward slowly. Captain Thain's left hand followed this manoeuvre until the throttles were in the fully open position. The plane was racing down the runway for its second attempt to take off when – *Whoah*. There it was again. A shuddering of the plane as the brakes were applied, the engines dropping their revs until the props were just ticking over.

We had stopped once more, halfway down the runway.

It was 14.35 hours and 20 seconds.

Everything was so smooth and well disciplined, almost as though it had just been a practice run. And now we were coasting towards the end of the runway.

We passengers sat back in consternation. Everything seemed to be going well. Why this second halt? Of course, we did not know that once again fluctuating boost pressures had caused the crew to abandon take-off.

Questions and answers were tossed about in the cabin until the voice of the stewardess, Miss Bellis, silenced all the theories. There was a slight mechanical fault and we were going back to the terminal buildings to have it rectified. They hoped to be able to take off soon, and we should hold ourselves in readiness for that recall.

As we squelched back across the tarmac, I was busy explaining to Duncan Edwards and Bobby Charlton that, no matter what the fault was, there was no danger. I understood there was a point of no return on the runway where, if the pilot was not happy about the plane, he could still pull up quite safely.

I looked up at the high wing of the Elizabethan monoplane as we passed, to see if ice on the wings had caused failures. There was nothing extraordinary in the fact that I should think of this as a possible cause. For five-and-a-half years in the war I had worked as an airframe fitter in the RAF, and any rigger on the flights would tell you ice on the wings was the first thing he looked for in conditions such as these.

The feeling that it could be ice forming on the wings and preventing the plane developing enough lift to get us in the air was driven more forcibly into my mind when I recalled a similar situation in Bilbao just thirteen months before. In January 1957 Manchester United flew there for a European Cup tie; and BEA flew a ground engineer out on his own, to make sure the plane was serviced correctly and that it was de-iced, for in that part of sunny (?) Spain there was snow. Why, we even took pictures of the Manchester United players sweeping the wings of the Dakota free of ice and a layer of snow before we took off for England.

With those thoughts racing through my mind, I looked hard at the high wing of the Elizabethan. Impossible from the ground to get a full view of the upper surface of the wing . . . But why was I concerned? The ground crews, when they refuelled, would have checked that, and it was thirteen years since I had serviced a plane; there were many more modern ideas now, heaters in the wings and all sorts of gadgets . . . First-class ground engineers would be servicing this machine; they would know what they were doing. So I swept those idle thoughts out of my mind and entered into the fug and fun in the lounge.

The comics, Frank Swift and Eric Thompson, had taken over. Eric, small and round, had picked up Big Swifty's overcoat and he was shuffling around the room like a lost grizzly bear, the coat almost trailing the floor, the arms hanging hugely by his sides. Big Swifty was trying to cram his massive torso into Eric's coat. 'Must have shrunk,' he was saying with that gormless grin so famed in the sporting world. 'Or maybe I've growed on this trip.'

Archie Ledbrooke was laughing. 'Anyone know any good hotels here in Munich, just in case they don't find what the trouble is and we have to stay overnight? Come to think of it, anyone got any spare German currency? I'm cleaned out of traveller's cheques. I spent up buying presents in Belgrade for my wife and daughters.'

Henry Rose was wandering from one group of people to the next, trying to discover if they had heard why we had stopped. 'We must get back tonight,' he said. 'It's the Press Ball in Manchester. I'm going into the office first, to finish my Postbag, although I've mopped up most of it already.' He waggled a bunch of papers. That was just like Henry. His Sports Postbag was a big selling item with the *Daily Express*; one of the secrets of his own phenomenal success. He carried it everywhere; on planes and trains – yes, even into the airport lounge in Munich.

Over the loudspeakers came a voice summoning us back to the airliner. I was surprised; it seemed only a few minutes since we had clattered down the steps to get off the plane. Chairs and tables scraped on the floor as the passengers stood up and headed for the door where Tom Curry stood to make sure no one had missed the message.

'Come on, Geoff . . . come on, Roger . . . Duncan . . . Eddie . . . Billy. We don't want to be kept here all night. All aboard now.'

Carefully, lest I might slip and break a leg, I squelched back across the tarmac with that nagging thought: 'They couldn't have de-iced in this short time. Must have been done before we left Belgrade, or maybe when we first landed. It certainly couldn't have been done in these past few minutes.'

As I reached the entrance hatch of the airliner, I caught sight of a reassuringly broad back which I thought must belong to the station engineer. There was obviously a technical discussion going on up there in the cockpit. Whatever the cause of those two abortive attempts to get up into the air, these chaps would have it under control now. So I pushed ahead into the plane, without any lingering doubts. Eric Thompson was just inside the door, putting his gear on the rack above the place where he was sitting. Once again I remarked: 'I'll come and join you as soon as we get off the deck.'

'I can hardly wait for the pleasure of your company,' he said with heavy sarcasm, giving me a playful push. 'Come on, Fatty, see you soon'.

'Excuse me.' I was trying to find a gap through the mass of humanity blocking the gangway; the card school were settling down again like a nest of chirpy sparrows.

I reached my place, some three seats in front of the bulkhead by the galley; beyond that was the radio officer's place and then the cockpit. The crew were just getting things in order as the station engineer left. Breathing heavily after that dash back to the plane, I pushed my coat on the rack above my head, along with my typewriter and the presents I was bringing home, grabbed the safety harness and clipped it in position. One last precaution before take-off, which I did as surreptitiously and as quickly as I could, was to remove my small dental plate. Don't laugh. I always did that. After all, I didn't want to risk swallowing that tiny plate if we had some slight collision or mishap, and I always slipped it back into place once we were in the air.

I half-turned in my seat, looking over my left shoulder to speak to Peter Howard. 'Pretty quick, don't you think, Pete?' I meant the ground crews must have done a snappy job to solve the technical fault which had kept us on the ground and get us serviceable to fly in perhaps a little over ten minutes. Peter Howard nodded.

'Everyone here?' The stewardess was making a last-minute check to see everyone was aboard. 'Blimey, we are one short.' Tom Curry checked his players; the stewardess checked the full passenger list.

At that moment the red-faced Alf Clarke hurried across the tarmac, puffing and panting, obviously upset that he had caused this delay.

'Come on, Alf . . . quick, man . . . Here comes Alf. Good old Alf . . . come on, we want to get off home.' The players were banteringly pulling his leg as Clarke dived aboard and started to fasten himself in.

'What are you so excited about? Anyone would think we were going somewhere special. I had to tell the office about the delay.

After all, we might have had to stay in Munich all night.'

'Oh blimey, don't say that, Alf!'

Alf Clarke had sent his story. The pilots were now told the missing passenger was aboard.

From the Elizabethan this radio message crackled to the control tower: 'Are we cleared to line up?'

It was 14.59 hours and 30 seconds.

We were just 4½ minutes from the disaster.

3 We Start Rolling . . . and then Tragedy Strikes

Flying is safer than driving a car, probably safer than crossing a busy road in rush hour. The difficulty is convincing many air passengers of that fact. You see them hurrying up the ramp to try and get their favourite seats aboard the aircraft, then anxiously fastening and unfastening their seat belts to get the correct position. Then you notice their hands whiten as they grip the arm rests for take-off, because it is in the take-off and the landing that most accidents occur.

Thus, over the years, I have been asked hundreds of times: 'What on earth made you get back on the aircraft after those two attempts to take off had failed. Didn't anyone have the guts to refuse to re-board the aircraft?'

I can only speak for myself. The thought of any possible danger never crossed my mind. On those first two runs I was quite convinced the pilots were playing safe, and that they had pulled up because they were concerned about the ice conditions. The pilot's life is just as much at risk as his passengers', so I was quite convinced that both Thain and Rayment had been reassured that the aeroplane was airworthy – and that it was perfectly safe to take off. Like all the other passengers, I settled down in my seat quite confident that in a few hours I would be sitting in the warmth and comfort of my home in Manchester, with my wife Peggy, and my sons Andrew and Alastair. No one seemed alarmed, indeed there were a few weak jokes about checking whether the pilot had got the elastic fully wound up ready for take-off. Once again we had the usual engine checks. Then the airliner started to roll away from the terminal buildings to the runway, the main wheels leaving twin tracks in the snow and slush.

We had reached that pregnant moment when passengers are waiting for the engines to roar into life, as the pilots wait for permission to take off. Our 'plane was coded ZULU UNIFORM

−609 (G–ALZU), and the signals between her and the control tower at Munich were tape-recorded like this:

Hrs	Mins	Secs	
14	56	30	*Elizabethan 609*: München Control Tower B–Line 609 Zulu Uniform – I am ready to taxi – Over.
			T.W.R.: 609 Zulu Uniform – München Tower, wind two nine zero – eight knots – cleared to runway two five – Q.N.H. one zero, zero four – Time five six and three quarters – Over.
14	56	50	*609*: Thank You.
14	59	30	*609*: Munich 609 Zulu Uniform – Are we cleared to line-up?
			T.W.R.: B–Line 609 Zulu Uniform – Cleared to line-up and hold. – And here is your clearance – Over.
			609: Roger – Go Ahead.
14	59	40	*T.W.R.*: München Control clears B–Line 609 to the Manchester Airport via route as filed – Maintain one seven thousand feet – right turn after take-off –climb on south course inbound Freising Range and maintain four thousand feet until further advised – Over.
15	00	00	*609*: ROGER – I understand. I am cleared to Manchester via the advised route to maintain seventeen thousand feet – a right turn out – the south course inbound to the Freising Range up to four thousand feet – maintain four until advised – Over.
			T.W.R.: ROGER – Clearance correct.
15	00	40	*T.W.R.*: B–Line 609 – What is your rate of climb? – Over.
15	00	50	*609*: Six hundred feet a minute.
			T.W.R.: Ah . . . ROGER.
15	02	00	*T.W.R.*: B–Line 609 – Your clearance void if not airborne by zero four. Time now zero two.

			609: Roger – Understand valid until zero four.
15	02	40	*609*: Ah, Munich – 609 Zulu Uniform is ready for take-off.
			T.W.R.: 609 – The wind three zero zero one zero knots – Cleared for take-off.
15	02	50	*609*: ROGER – Thank you.
15	03	06	*609*: ROLLING.
15	03	10	*T. W. R.*: Nich Tower – ROGER.

None of this cryptic technical information which passed between the air controllers and the pilots was heard by the Manchester United party. We were fidgeting, waiting to get airborne, completely unaware of this conversation between pilots and control tower.

It was about two years later, when I had time to read the official German report on the accident, that I had the opportunity to study this tape-recorded message. I have pondered over that message from the control tower at two minutes past three o'clock, which informed Thain and Rayment that they had exactly two minutes to make up their minds whether they were ready to take off for Manchester; otherwise, for a third time, they would have been forced to delay the return home. I wonder what went through their minds then? Did they feel under pressure? If they didn't get the aircraft airborne within the next two minutes, they might face a much longer delay on the ground.

In the passengers' cabin, we didn't know the pilots had been warned they had two minutes to make up their minds whether or not to go. As we hadn't eaten since breakfast, I know that personally I was looking forward to the meal we had been promised would be served on the second half of the journey from Munich to Manchester.

Suddenly, there was a thunderous roar as the engines burst into life. I listened intently. Not a cough or a splutter, as the motors throbbed louder and louder, until they had reached their familiar high pitched whine . . . then we started to move. Slowly at first, then faster and faster, racing down the runway like a high powered car . . . 70 knots, 80 . . . 90 . . . 100 knots an hour.

Those were the figures which flashed before the expert eyes of

Commander James Thain as he monitored the instruments. He saw the needle reach 117, then as he told the official German enquiry into the accident . . . the needle inexplicably dropped back to 105 . . . What the hell had gone wrong again? For the first time on that fatal run, he allowed his eyes to look up from his instruments and realised the airliner was running out of runway! In that nerve shattering split second he heard his co-pilot, Captain Ken Rayment, cry out:

'Christ . . . we are not going to make it.'

By this time, even we passengers realised something had gone drastically wrong.

Peter Howard says he thought he heard the starboard engine make a noise like a car changing gear. Harry Gregg had the same impression. Sitting as I was on the other side of the aeroplane from these two, I didn't notice any change in the note of the engine. But I was now becoming slightly alarmed at the huge wave of slush being thrown backwards by the port wheel, as we ploughed along that runway. We zipped past a red building away to my right, which I remember quite clearly because of its prominent colour, and the fact that on our two previous runs, we had slowed and stopped almost opposite this landmark.

I was sure we had already gone past the point of no return, although it was quite impossible, because of that wave of brownish slush, to make out whether or not the wheels had actually left the ground.

Dennis Viollet and Bobby Charlton were seated in front of me, so I tried to shout to make myself heard above the roar of the engines: 'Have the wheels gone up yet . .?'

There was no reply. They couldn't have heard my question, so I leaned over as far as my safety belt would allow, to look through the porthole, with my head craning to try and see what lay in front of us.

My heart froze when I saw the perimeter fence rushing towards us. Like Ken Rayment, I knew in that chilling split second that we were not going to make it.

I felt the machine suddenly lurch off the concrete runway to the right, onto the grass, with the landing lights flashing by. I felt a sickening blow behind the left ear, the kind of friendly cuff big, strong Frank Swift was fond of administering to his friends. But this wasn't Swifty having some fun, this was a real thwack. I could feel my senses slipping away. Then there was a horrendous bang, and in my dazed state I thought I saw the port wheel crashing through a crumpled fuselage. The bulkhead behind me was caving in, with cases and other items of luggage hurtling around in the cabin.

There was a kind of green haze sweeping up in front of my eyes, like a huge tidal wave engulfing me. Everything was becoming hazy, even though I kept shaking my head in a desperate attempt to stay conscious; I was like a drowning man fighting to keep his head above water. I had never been knocked out in my life, and I was fighting against that awful feeling of just fading into oblivion.

This couldn't be happening to me. This was crazy. I could hear, as though far away in the distance, a tremendous rending and grinding of metal, and it was only when the airliner started to buck like a wild thing that I realised it was our aeroplane which was being ripped apart, as it slid helplessly along the ground. There was a tremendous hammering on the fuselage near my head, as though a giant was getting to work with a sledgehammer . . . Then mercifully my eyes closed.

Further down the fuselage, Matt Busby also felt the machine make that sudden lurch to the right. Up went his hands to protect his face. Then he too lost consciousness. I believe we two were lucky that we did pass out. Otherwise the memories might have been much harsher to bear.

There was, perhaps, only one man who lived through every nightmarish moment of that tragedy until the day he died, and that was Captain James Thain. When he saw that needle drop back from 117 knots an hour, he banged furiously on the throttle to try and coax more power out of the two engines, to give us enough power to get off the ground. The throttle levers were in the fully forward position. Nothing could save us now.

The glittering Elizabethan aeroplane, so elegant and comfortable to fly in, was now little more than an aluminium tomb – out of control, ploughing through every obstacle in its path, as both pilots fought desperately to avoid the imminent disaster.

Beyond the perimeter fence, outside the bounds of the airfield, there was a house, which in normal circumstances was not a hazard for an orthodox take-off. As Zulu Uniform plunged past the landing lights, it was clear to both pilots that emergency action was needed. Thain pulled the lever to retract the undercarriage, as Rayment slammed on the brakes.

Too late. Zulu Uniform raced across the 250 yards of the grass stopway beyond the concrete runway, smashed through the fence and hit the house; the port wing, only a few feet from me, was torn off, leaving our aeroplane like a huge wounded bird, clattering and bumping along the ground completely out of control. About 100 yards further on, the right side of the fuselage, just behind the one good wing, sliced into a wooden hut standing on a concrete base. The impact tore off the rear part of the plane just behind the starboard wing, which careered off on its own before coming to rest.

By now, what was left of the undercarriage had been torn away, and this left the front of the airliner, still with that starboard wing attached to the fuselage, slithering and screeching along on its belly, the wing carving great chunks out of the trees in its path like a giant scythe. This part of the wreckage, in which I was strapped, was spinning round helplessly in circles.

As it did so, a number of passengers, including some of the team, were thrown out into the snow. What was once a sleek aeroplane was now a smouldering ruin, leaving a trail of death and destruction in its wake. Less than a minute previously I had been sitting in the company of the Young Kings of British Soccer, laughing and joking in the full flush of their athletic prowess. Now they lay dead . . . or dying . . . or brutally injured and dumbly shocked by the tragedy which had hit them.

With them in the snow was their manager Matt Busby, still, like Bobby Charlton, strapped in his seat. They, like me, were among the lucky ones.

The final tape-recorded message from the stricken airliner to the control tower says all that needs to be said at this stage: '15 hrs 04 mins 00 seconds: Munich from B-Line Zulu Unif . . .' Then the message stopped abruptly. It was 54 seconds from the time we started rolling joyously down the runway until disaster struck.

We survivors didn't realise it at the time, but as our aircraft was tearing down the runway, we were being followed by a fleet of ambulances and rescue crews. Within a few minutes of their arrival at the crash, Press cables were crackling over the wires: 'MANCHESTER UNITED PLANE CRASHES AT MUNICH . . . STILL SEARCHING FOR SURVIVORS.'

4 Salute to the Brave

I do not know how long I lay there trapped in the wreckage. It could only have been minutes, yet every second became an eternity, and I now realise how easy it could have been for my life to tick away, as did those of so many of my friends.

I have no recollection of fear, more of angry frustration, because I seemed unable to move, and every breath I took was agony. I kept trying to breathe in deeply, to clear my senses, and yet every time I did so, I was aware of stabbing pains in my chest. Every so often my senses cleared, and I have a very clear picture of lying trapped in all the tangled metal, looking towards the tail of the aeroplane – only there was no tail or rudder there. I could see a gap, and through it the dull grey sky with fluttering ice flakes. Don't ask me why, but in that moment my mind suddenly flipped back to an incident more than a year previously, when a Viscount coming in to land at Ringway in Manchester, from Amsterdam, had crashed into some houses when the bolt retaining the flap sheared, causing the wing to dip and the aeroplane to lose height with fatal results. It had been a big story at the time, and I remembered how, when it happened, I had wondered what flashed through the minds of the passengers in those last fatal seconds before death and injury struck them. I looked at the chaos around me . . . So this was what it was like . . . what a silly bloody way to die . . . Then blackness swept over me again.

I was lucky to pass out, completely oblivious of the frantic activity around me, and unaware that the plane was in danger of blowing up in a sheet of flame. A man's first thought in a crisis is to save himself, and yet there were brave men on that tragic airfield who were ready to risk their own lives to save those of their comrades.

One of them was Peter Howard. When our airliner ripped into that house, the impact sent the *Daily Mail* photographer cartwheeling through the air. As a bulkhead caved in, luggage and bodies were hurtling through the air inside the cabin, as though thrown by a huge cocktail shaker. Howard thrust out a protective arm to prevent a suitcase from thudding into his face. He landed on his hands and knees, as the front part of the aircraft spun round and round in maddening circles, until she stopped, just a crumpled heap of metal, with a pall of murky black smoke billowing up from it to mark its last resting place.

Back in the airfield buildings, the administrative staff watched thunderstruck, as the fire engines and ambulances came clanging down the runway to the rescue. Inside the wreckage of Zulu Uniform, Peter Howard stirred, surprised to find himself still alive and able to move. His first thought was to get away as fast as he could. On his right, he could see the shocked face of his colleague Ted Ellyard.

'Are you all right, Ted?' he shouted.

'I think so, mate,' came the reply.

Immediately Howard started to scramble through the broken spars and twisted metal to a hole in the fuselage. Fear gave him added strength as he tore at the debris to get out, because the stench of petrol was a frightening reminder that, at any moment, the petrol tanks could blow up like a fireball.

Once he had fought his way clear, Howard had only one thought: 'I knew I was OK,' he told me afterwards, 'and all I wanted to do was run away as fast as I could from the terrible carnage around me.' Had he done so, who could have blamed him?

In the cockpit, Captain James Thain hurriedly unfastened his seat belt. In the adjacent seat, Captain Rayment also tried to free himself. He was muttering to himself: 'Are my passengers all right?' That seemed to be his only concern. Thain shouted at him: 'Come on man!'

It was no use. Rayment's legs were jammed in the wreckage of the pedals and, suddenly realising this, Thain shouted, 'Hang on, Ken, we'll get you out.' Rayment didn't reply; he had fallen into a deep coma.

Thain knew his drill: to get those passengers who were capable of moving themselves away from the stricken aircraft with all possible speed.

As he jumped down from the cockpit, he waved away

Howard, Ellyard, Harry Gregg and others, shouting at them, 'Get away . . . go on, run . . . get away!' Then he and the radio officer, George Rogers, grabbed fire extinguishers and started trying to put out four or five small fires around the aircraft.

Common sense should have made the survivors obey Thain's command to flee the wreck, but now that Harry Gregg had recovered his wits, he was furious. He stood on a little hummock of ground shouting, 'Come on, lads, let's get stuck in. There are some people still inside the plane.'

Gregg didn't wait for the others; ignoring the threat of fire, he bravely wormed his way back into the wreck, to search for survivors. Within a few moments he re-appeared, holding a tiny bundle. It was the 20 months-old baby daughter of Mrs Vera Lukic, wife of the Yugoslavian air attaché in London, who was being allowed to travel back on United's charter plane to England.

The baby's face was badly swollen and bruised, but the little mite was alive. She was breathing, she wasn't going to die. Today that baby is a lovely young woman, although, sadly, a series of operations failed to save the sight of one of her eyes.

Peter Howard, Ted Ellyard and the two hostesses, Margaret Bellis and Rosemary Cheverton, joined Gregg, one of the hostesses tenderly taking the baby in her arms; then the United goalkeeper went back inside the wreckage. This time he brought Mrs Lukic herself to safety.

Naturally, as soon as she saw her baby was safe, Mrs Lukic gave a cry of relief; sobbing she was helped over the snow by Peter Howard, to be re-united with that precious bundle.

All the survivors who escaped unaided are agreed about the nightmare quality of the terrible sights that met their eyes. Bobby Charlton – then a fresh-faced teenager – who had been sitting in front of me, was thrown clear, and incredibly was found, dazed and shocked but still strapped in his seat, some 70 yards away from the wreckage.

Jackie Blanchflower recovered consciousness to find a team-mate lying across him. His pal was not breathing.

When the plane crashed, Bill Foulkes was playing a game of cards with Albert Scanlon. Afterwards, Bill told me: 'I just could not believe what was happening. One moment I was looking at the cards in my hand; the next moment the tail seemed to fall away in front of me, and I was looking up at the sky. I couldn't see where Albert Scanlon had got to. Then I heard a voice: it was the pilot, Thain, screaming at everyone to get the hell out of it, in case the plane caught fire and exploded. I took that as an order, so I ran as fast as I could until I found myself on a road with a group of Germans. I couldn't tell what they were saying, because they were all chattering wildly. Then I looked down at my feet and noticed, for the first time, that I had run through all that snow and slush completely unaware that I was not wearing any shoes! When we got back on the plane for the take-off, I had taken them off to feel more comfortable, and had run all this way without them!

'I think this discovery brought me to my senses. For the first time I noticed smoke hanging over the wreckage, and I realised we had crashed and that my mates were still over there; so I ran back to see what help I could give. The Germans couldn't believe that I was actually a survivor myself.'

When he retraced his steps Foulkes found Matt Busby, in his seat on the ground, painfully trying to push himself up with one hand. Busby was icy cold, as though the fingers of death were already upon him, so Foulkes and Gregg vigorously rubbed his hands and back to try to revive him until more expert help arrived.

All around were bodies, some injured, some dead. Howard and Ellyard, realising there were still people trapped in the wreckage, went back to see what succour they could bring. They found Ray Wood, understudy to Harry Gregg, groaning in pain and unable to move, because he was pinned by part of the undercarriage. Partly across him lay Albert Scanlon, trapped by bits of metal and the team's basket containing their playing kit. Inch by inch, Howard and Ellyard cleared the debris until they could get Scanlon and Wood outside, leaving them to the care of the ambulancemen and nurses. Then they resumed their search for more survivors.

'There's some one else here,' shouted Ellyard. Howard joined him. 'It's Frank Taylor,' he said.

I could not have been a pretty sight: the left side of my head had been sliced open, creating a wound that eventually needed 21 stitches; I was breathing with difficulty as a result of a double fracture of the collar bone and nine broken ribs; my left arm hung helplessly from a smashed elbow joint; and my right leg above the ankle was crushed, with the foot bent backwards to expose the broken tibia and fibula protruding through the dark grey cloth of the trouser leg. As gently as they could, Howard and Ellyard pulled me outside the aircraft. Howard was trying to comfort me, but I just stared at them without saying a word. My senses had flown, so I do not know who put me on the stretcher, but I do remember quite clearly trying to sit up on it, and Harry Gregg coming over to push me gently in the chest.

'Don't worry Frank, you are going to be all right,' he said. I didn't know what he was talking about. Then I noticed I had a cigarette in my mouth, and I remembered I had, on my wife's advice, recently stopped smoking. I looked idly at my suit and noticed it was covered in mud and slush.

'My God,' I thought, 'what would Peggy say if she saw this? Me starting to smoke again! And look at my suit, what would she say about the mess on my new suit?' Then I looked down, and saw that my right foot appeared to be almost severed, with blood oozing out. I'm no hero. I passed out at that point.

The real heroes were still risking their lives looking for survivors. Howard, now assisted by Radio Officer Rogers, made one last sortie.

In the wreckage, a white shirt attracted their notice. It was a young man, his chest heaving very slowly, trying to gasp in air. That young man was Ken Morgans, an 18-year-old Welsh lad, who had been given his big chance in the European Cup tie in Belgrade. He had left England just four days previously, overjoyed and full of hope that maybe one day he would be hailed by the Welsh as another Billy Meredith. Incredibly the pink boyish face had not been damaged or marked by the heaped jumble of wood and metal around his head. He was unconscious, and pinned by a spar. Howard and Rogers got a crowbar to ease this away, so that Morgans too could join the list of survivors.

The starboard engine still smouldered, but the firefighters now had this under control. Quite clearly the prompt action of Thain and Rogers had averted the very real threat of the whole aircraft going up in smoke.

At last Peter Howard could do no more. Although he had no devastating physical injury, the shock and the horror he had suffered were now taking their toll. As he wandered aimlessly from the wreck, trying to gather his thoughts, he saw a forlorn crumpled figure lying on the ground. Tenderly he lifted the head and recognised Roger Byrne, United's young captain, one of the most stylish left backs ever to play for England. The lean, handsome face was unmarked, nor was there any trace of injury on that beautifully tapered athletic body. Roger Byrne might have been sleeping; but Peter Howard knew instinctively that he was dead. He was not the only great international footballer to lose his life that day. Nor was the spectre of Roger Byrne, lying lifeless in the snow, the only grim sight Peter Howard had to endure.

Peter Howard has a very special place in my life. We newspaper people live in a very competitive world, but I like to think we are also a brotherhood. It is not an easy life, and sometimes we cocoon our real feelings in a covering of cynicism.

Just how much Peter Howard suffered, he has kept assiduously to himself. It was his mournful task to tell the other newspapers that all the other sports writers apart from Frank Taylor had been killed. Because of his newspaper experience and background, he was able to file all the early stories and descriptions of the crash. He was fulsome in his praise for the bravery of Harry Gregg, Ted Ellyard, the stewardesses, the Captain, James Thain, and the Radio Officer, George Rogers. One name he omitted from those dispatches, and that was the name of Peter Howard.

When he dragged me from the scene of carnage I was semi-conscious, but some fifteen weeks after the accident, apart from my broken bones, I was very much alive when Captain Thain called in to the Rechts der Isar Hospital in Munich, to find out how I was getting along. We didn't discuss the air crash in great detail, but when I mentioned the name of Peter Howard Captain Thain said briefly and with great feeling, 'GOD! That chap has some guts!'

I'll second that remark!

5 Achtung! Achtung!

Professor Georg Maurer, Chief Surgeon at the Rechts der Isar Hospital in Munich, walked briskly along the corridor of Station 1 on the fourth floor of the building. It was in this area that his own private patients were situated, and he was on his afternoon rounds checking their progress. The hands of the clock on the wall pointed to 3.15 in the afternoon.

The Professor and his surgical teams had been busy since 7.30 that morning in the operating theatres, grouped tidily just down the corridor beyond the frosted glass doors marked 'OPERA-TION SALLES'.

The Professor, a shortish, roly-poly figure of a man, had taken his share of the 25 operations which had been performed that day yet, despite those long hours of concentrated work, he showed little sign of fatigue. He moved quickly from bed to bed, the warm brown eyes twinkling mischievously behind his rimless spectacles, having a quick word with his patients in that friendly efficient way that Matt Busby and myself were soon to know. Hurrying along behind him came a posse of white coated figures: Herr Doktor Opelt, his chief aide, Herr Doktor Gross, a young trainee and the Chief Nursing Sister in the hospital, a nun, Sister Maria Gilda.

As the Professor and his team bustled out of Room 405, a tiny black-haired nursing orderly, Maria Spitzener, came running excitedly out of Sister Gilda's private office, shouting 'Herr Professor, Herr Professor, telefon!'

From the urgency in the girl's voice, Maurer knew this was something serious; he hurried to pick up the receiver. As he listened the warm smile left his face, and he spoke loudly so that his staff could hear:

'Ja . . . ja . . . Flugzeut catastrophe at Reim . . .'

Once they heard the word catastrophe, Maurer's assistants raced to their emergency stations. They knew the drill, because

Maurer was not only an excellent surgeon, he was also a brilliant organiser, and he had prepared them for an emergency such as this. On the hellfire beaches at Dunkirk 18 years previously, Maurer had been decorated with the Iron Cross for saving the lives of British as well as German soldiers. That and similar wartime experiences had taught him the need for a well-planned emergency service to deal with casualties, and one of his first duties when appointed head of the Rechts der Isar Hospital was to set up medical teams to deal with any air crash victims.

As one of those victims, I was only aware of being in some kind of crowded mini-bus, which seemed to be ignoring all known speed limits as it bumped and bounced over fields on to a road. I was not fully conscious, but whenever I came to, I tried to struggle to get up, only to find myself forcibly restrained. I heard someone – I think it was Billy Foulkes – say, 'Don't worry, Frank. Just lie still. You're going to be all right.'

I still had terrible difficulty in breathing, and then suddenly, for the first time, I felt a searing pain shoot up my right leg. I could not understand why it should be hurting so much, and as I was being held down, I could not see what had happened. The pain became so great that I was only too pleased when I saw someone I took to be a doctor come towards me brandishing a hypodermic syringe. 'Ssh,' he said. 'This will put you to sleep.'

Frankly I had got past caring, and raised no complaint when he tore the sleeve of my jacket, and then ripped my shirt to expose my arm. As the needle plunged into my arm, I felt so terribly, terribly weary. My eyes started to flicker, then they closed. I was really happy to be falling asleep. Perhaps I would wake up and find this was just a horrible dream.

Fortunately for the crash survivors, the staff at the Rechts der Isar were a hive of activity. The staccato commands ripped out over the hospital's inter communications system: 'Achtung! Achtung! Herr Professor Kessel . . . Herr Professor Thysinger . . . Herr Doktor Lechner . . . Frau Doktor Schmidt . . . Frau Doktor Jacques . . .' All these specialists, doctors, nurses and theatre sisters sprang into action. The Blood Bank was alerted, male nurses and orderlies had trolleys and stretchers ready to deal with the injured. There was no panic. Just organised efficiency. Those who work in hospitals and at casualty stations dare not allow normal sensitive emotions to deflect them from their duty. They feel these emotions, like the rest of us, but when an emergency like this one occurs and lives are at risk, they have to work at speed, each person carrying out an allotted task. They act as a team, realising that one weak link puts a patient's life at risk.

Maurer, as I was to learn, was a born leader. And on this tragic day, his only concern was to get his team working with the controlled speed for which he had trained them. He had learned from his wartime experiences how to deal with cases of severe shock and how to get his team working efficiently. To give a true picture of the kind of man Maurer was, he actually appointed extra electricians to man all the lifts, just in case an electrical fault caused a lift bearing a critically injured patient to jam between floors. That was Maurer: a surgeon, recognised internationally as a man of extraordinary ability, who also possessed this remarkable ability for organisation down to the minutest detail.

Maurer and his team didn't have long to wait. Police cars were already clanging their way through the streets of Munich, carving a clear path through the slush for the ambulances which followed.

Snowflakes fluttered down from leaden skies, as Germans on the pavements gazed in wonder at this fleet of ambulances and police cars. Obviously it was an accident of some kind, but they didn't know then that this was an air crash involving a famous soccer team, and that on the morrow the name of Munich would be emblazoned once more across the world's newspapers. This time, it would not be a story of political intrigue like Hitler's evil scheming in the 1938 Munich Settlement. This was a life and death drama which tugged at the heart strings because so many young and famous sportsmen were involved.

'Achtung! Achtung!' The ambulances hurtled through the gates and slithered to a halt outside the Casualty Department.

Among the waiting medical specialists was Professor Frank Kessel, head of the neuro-surgical department. As he told me later, his heart sank as the ambulances screeched to a stop. The crash survivors were slid out on stretchers and rushed inside . . . most of them looked very young. This was the list of casualties:

DUNCAN EDWARDS:	Manchester United and England left-half – mortally injured.
KEN RAYMENT:	co-pilot – mortally injured.
FRANK SWIFT:	soccer correspondent for the *News of the World* and former England and Manchester City goalkeeper – mortally injured.
JOHNNY BERRY:	Manchester United and England outside-right – in a deep coma with a fractured skull and other injuries.
MATT BUSBY:	manager of Manchester United – seriously ill with chest crushed and broken foot.
FRANK TAYLOR:	northern sports columnist of the *News Chronicle* – seriously injured with 21 fractures.
ALBERT SCANLON:	Manchester United outside-left – left leg badly injured, and his scalp gashed.
DENNIS VIOLLET:	Manchester United inside-right – head injuries and shock.
BOBBY CHARLTON:	Manchester United inside-left – head injury and shock.
JACKIE BLANCHFLOWER:	Manchester United and Northern Ireland centre-half – fractured arm and pelvis.
RAY WOOD:	Manchester United goalkeeper – head and leg injuries.
KEN MORGANS:	Manchester United outside-right – head injury and severe shock.
MRS MIKLOS:	wife of the travel agent who was killed – quickly taken to Stoke Mandeville hospital in England.
MRS LUKIC:	taken with her baby daughter to another hospital where they both recovered, although the baby lost the sight of one eye.

Professor Frank Kessel saw Frank Swift and me lying on adjacent stretchers. We were both bleeding from the mouth. Kessel didn't then know who I was, but when Germany invaded Austria in 1938, he had left his native Vienna and eventually made his way to Manchester where he worked for several years. An avid sportsman himself, he had become a keen follower of football, and now he quickly recognised Swift as the former England and Manchester City goalkeeper. Then he caught sight of Matt Busby, the very clever Scottish half back he had seen playing for Liverpool and Manchester City before the outbreak of World War II.

'Das ist ein Englische Fussball spiel,' he shouted to his medical colleagues. This was how the hospital staff learned that the victims of the air crash were from an English football team.

Kessel told me later that at first they did not think Big Swifty was badly injured, but he died on being carried into the hospital. A post mortem examination revealed that the main aorta artery had been severed, apparently by his seat belt.

Less than 30 minutes after Zulu Uniform had started its last fatal take-off attempt, the seriously injured were all in hospital. The heroes and heroines who had acted so promptly to save our lives – Harry Gregg, Peter Howard, Ted Ellyard, Bill Foulkes, Captain Thain, Radio Officer Rogers and the two stewardesses, Margaret Bellis and Rosemary Cheverton, were also admitted to hospital for medical examination. Shock, grievous shattering shock, after what they had seen, was writ large on their faces, as Professor Maurer and his Angels of Mercy set to work.

6   I am Reported Killed

I was lying, so I was told later, on a stretcher, with my chest bared and the name Andrew MacDonald scrawled in red across the upper part of my body. Like Matt Busby, who was on an adjacent stretcher, I had difficulty in breathing.

Professor Maurer and his staff quickly ordered five of the critically injured to be taken upstairs to the intensive care unit. They were Matt Busby, Duncan Edwards, Ken Rayment, Johnny Berry and myself.

About the time that we were being whisked upstairs in the lift, my wife Peggy was at home preparing tea. My two little sons, Andrew and Alastair, were running round, continually asking her, 'How long before Dad comes home?' They were excited, because my work as a sports writer on the *News Chronicle* meant that it was often after midnight before I finished; I didn't get many opportunities to have tea with my family. As my wife scurried round the kitchen, the telephone rang. It startled her, but her first thought was that our plane had landed earlier than scheduled and that she would have to speed up her preparations for the meal.

As she picked up the receiver, she heard the voice of Tom Simms, the northern sports editor of the *News Chronicle*. He tried desperately to sound normal as he told my wife that Manchester United's plane had crashed, but that there were a number of survivors and I was among them. That news flash, that I was alive, had been sent by Peter Howard, but in those early hours after the tragedy the full extent of my injuries was not known.

Tom Simms assured my wife that I was safe in hospital, and that he would keep in constant touch with her as more information came in. He added that if there was anything further that either he or his staff could do to help her in this emergency, she had only to ask.

My wife, of course, was not the only wife in Manchester that day to suffer the agony of not knowing how badly her husband was injured. The wives, mothers and sweethearts of all the players and sports writers were each caught up in their own fear.

A chill of hysteria gripped the city of Manchester. The first indication that something was wrong was recorded in the 'Stop Press' of the early afternoon editions of the *Manchester Evening News* and *Manchester Evening Chronicle*, when newsboys dashed along the streets shouting, 'Manchester United plane held up in Munich blizzard!' It was the kind of story that would attract United soccer fans, knowing that if the team didn't get home in time to play their Saturday League match against Wolves they would be heavily fined and censured. It served to reinforce the view of many soccer fans in those days, who thought Manchester United were crazy to play these European matches hundreds of miles away, instead of concentrating on the home Cup and League programme.

Hardly had the story of the delay hit the streets, than a more dreadful one was substituted: MANCHESTER UNITED IN PLANE CRASH. The entire city was stunned by the news. A group of United fans had already gathered at Ringway airport to give a victorious welcome to the team, their cheers now reduced to shocked silence; as the story stuttered over the teleprinters editors called emergency conferences to change the front page; and crowds clustered round newspaper sellers, not only in Manchester but in every city, town and village in the land.

Housewives, tuning in to their daily ration of 'Mrs Dale', were shattered when an announcer broke into the programme to report the news of the air crash. Men and women wept unashamedly on the street. It was, as one newspaper executive told me years later, an event like the assassination of President Kennedy, a tragedy which touched all sectors of the community, whether or not they were football fans. For those with loved ones on that plane it was a crisis one hopes they will never have to live through again.

We men like to think of ourselves as the tougher sex. We may be stronger physically, but in facing up to heart-rending human tragedies like this, many women are much more logical and practical. My wife certainly was. She didn't know whether I was going to live or die, but there were others to consider; so, after her conversation with Tom Simms, she put the receiver down to let the news sink in, and also to steady her nerves. Then she telephoned to my eldest brother Bill in Barrow-in-Furness, to explain what had happened and to ask him to let my 78-year-old mother know about the accident, in case she heard the news over the radio or TV, when the shock would be far greater.

My children, seeing the news flash on television, wanted to know what had happened. My wife explained in a matter-of-fact voice that Daddy had been slightly injured and that she might have to go out to Munich to nurse him and bring him back. The boys were content with that reply.

In Leeds, my eldest sister Vi, an officer in the Salvation Army, heard the news on radio and immediately telephoned my wife, not knowing whether I was alive or dead. She caught the first available train to Manchester to comfort my wife and give her all the help she needed. Vi was only one of many kind people that day; the telephone and the front door bell hardly stopped ringing as friends and neighbours offered their help.

All too slowly and agonisingly the news from Munich filtered through and the death-roll mounted:

Roger Byrne . . . Eddie Colman . . . Tommy Taylor . . . Tom Curry . . . Bert Whalley . . . Geoff Bent . . . Willie Satinoff . . . David Pegg . . . Billy Whelan . . . Mr Miklos . . . Mark Jones. It was unbelievable, this mournful unfolding of the tragedy, in which so many young footballers perished.

In the newspaper offices it soon became apparent that journalism too had suffered the most savage blow ever in the history of our profession. Newspapermen are used to recording tragedies; it is a thankless part of the job, and sometimes one gets a little too cynical. This was different, more personal; all these journalists were well-known men, well liked . . . they were colleagues. There were tears in the news-rooms as the appalling list grew. By 8 p.m. it was clear beyond all doubt that these eight journalists had died on duty:

Alf Clarke, *Manchester Evening Chronicle*
Don Davies, *Manchester Guardian*
George Follows, *Daily Herald*
Tom Jackson, *Manchester Evening News*

Archie Ledbrooke, *Daily Mirror*
Henry Rose, *Daily Express*
Frank Swift, *News of the World*
Eric Thompson, *Daily Mail*

They had died at the peak of their powers and their fame. Sadly the obituaries were prepared. Mine too. For everyone knew the Press lads flew all together, as a team.

Despite the early optimistic reports that I was safe and well, no further confirmation had come through. There was no Frank Taylor listed among the survivors . . . just a mysterious Andrew MacDonald, believed to be a member of the crew.

It was quite true that Peter Howard and Billy Foulkes had rung Manchester immediately after the accident to say that I had been dragged out alive but gravely injured. Since then, SILENCE. No one was quite sure just what had happened to the missing journalist Frank Taylor.

At home my wife tried to keep her frayed nerves under control as the hours unwound. As bulletin followed bulletin, even the usually optimistic Tom Simms began to lose hope. As the clock moved inexorably on he was forced to say: 'Don't hope too much now, Peggy . . . but if there is anything at all we can do . . .'

He knew. My wife knew. I always sat with my Press colleagues.

As women do, she clung to one faint slender hope. That name Andrew MacDonald among the survivors nagged her mind. No one seemed to know much about him.

My eldest son's name is Andrew MacDonald Taylor after my Scottish forebears. The boy's name was in my passport.

My wife breathed a prayer. Was it just possible? Could I have been thrown out of the plane, or my passport partly destroyed with only the name Andrew MacDonald legible, with the surname Taylor either torn or burnt off? Was it too silly to hope thus? That the Germans in their haste to attend the injured had seized on that remnant of passport and issued the name of Andrew MacDonald as a survivor?

No, it couldn't be true . . . it was too crazy . . . but it was worth a try. With her heart thumping she rang Tom Simms and spoke of her slim hope. Only too anxious to help, he set the wheels in motion. He contacted Munich as my wife telephoned BEA.

The airline said no crew member called Andrew MacDonald was on the plane, and so far as they knew, there was no passenger by that name either . . . unless Mr Busby or the Manchester United party had allowed an extra passenger called Andrew MacDonald to travel with them from Munich.

That was a glimmer of light. By now squads of German police were scouring the wreckage; sifting the debris to see if they could find Frank Taylor.

Late that night in the operating theatre of the Rechts der Isar Hospital a short stocky man stirred. On his chest, hastily scrawled in red, was the name Andrew MacDonald. Since early afternoon he had had only fleeting moments of consciousness and to all enquiries he insisted he was Andrew MacDonald.

He was troublesome when he did come round, struggling with the nurses and doctors at his bedside. Now as he moved an English-speaking German doctor questioned him yet again. 'Yes . . . my name is Frank Taylor,' he whispered.

The perspiring medical team sighed. The missing survivor had been found. The news was phoned to the *News Chronicle* in Manchester and from Tom Simms to my wife. 'Isn't that just like him,' she said with relief. 'Can't even remember his own name now.' Tom Simms, who had been sweating more than somewhat himself these past few hours, heartily agreed. In the newspaper composing rooms the obituaries were neatly in the pages. The presses were ready to start running when the news came – Frank Taylor's obituary was not needed that night. In the Brotherhood of the Press they were rather glad that one journalist was still alive; and they were only bitterly sorry that the obituaries of the other Press lads couldn't be taken out of the pages that terrible night. They kept mine handy just in case, although they hoped it would not be needed in the days to follow.

It was a fantastic thing that I should give my son's name to the hospital staff. The doctors in Munich thought that I probably shouted the boy's name as I was hit on the head and lost consciousness . . . and that this name was mirrored in my mind in those few dazed hours in the hospital, for I kept insisting I was Andrew MacDonald.

Some weeks later Professor Maurer recalled the incident,

which he thought was very funny. 'You caused us much worry, Mr Taylor. We have accounted for all the people but Frank Taylor. Mrs Taylor is worried, we are worried, the police are worried; and they are looking for Frank Taylor on the airfield. They cannot find him for he is sleeping peacefully here in my operating theatre . . . this is very naughty of you.' He beamed boyishly and fairly rocked with laughter.

'Sorry, Professor,' I replied as meekly as I could. 'I wasn't feeling quite myself when they brought me in here.'

But I am racing ahead of the story.

As soon as my wife knew her slender hope had become reality she was naturally overwhelmed with relief. She sat down with my sister to make plans for joining the Mercy Flight which BEA had organised to fly the relatives out to the injured. It was now well past midnight; the plane was due to leave Ringway at 9 am; she couldn't eat, she couldn't sleep, but she rested as best she could, while my brother Bill came speeding through the night from Barrow-in-Furness to give her support on that plane. Eighteen hours after the crash the relatives were flying to Munich via Paris.

On board that Viscount which left Ringway were Mrs Jean Busby, her son Sandy and her daughter Sheena with her husband Don Gibson, the Sheffield Wednesday footballer. There were other relatives of the injured on board. With them, too, sat Jimmy Murphy.

Murphy, the mercurial Welshman who had been Matt Busby's right-hand man for some thirteen years; who had helped to build this great football team; who had been out there on the football field coaching many of them when they were little more than schoolboys.

Murphy would have been in the crash but for an extraordinary chain of circumstances. He was due to go to Belgrade with Matt Busby as he so frequently did in the European Cup games. His place was booked, and then, at the last moment, he stepped down. As he was also team manager of the Welsh international side, he was needed with them in Cardiff for a World Cup match against Israel on the same day Manchester United played in Belgrade, Bert Whalley had taken Murphy's seat in the Elizabethan alongside Matt Busby – and Bert had been killed.

So Murphy, one of the gayest, most talkative men in football, sat silently brooding, the heartache locked up inside him, and like the rest on that aeroplane close to tears.

No one knew quite what they would find when they got to Munich. They had nothing to cling to but hope. That, and their prayers.

7 Back from the Valley of the Shadows

My wife Peggy tiptoed into the main operating theatre at the Rechts der Isar Hospital just after 6 pm on the Friday night, some 27 hours after the crash, hoping for the best but fearing the worst.

With her, was my eldest brother Bill. They found me lying half asleep in the dimly lit theatre, with a tube connected to my left foot and another apparently clamped to my nose, while in a bed nearby, under a plastic oxygen tent, lay Matt Busby.

'How is he? What are the chances?' my wife asked of the pretty woman doctor who had kept vigil by my bed for many hours. She held her arms out, like a balance, waggling them up and down. 'Fifty-fifty,' she said. 'He is strong, but he has pneumonia. The next few hours are vital.'

The news about Matt Busby was grim. Jean Busby was told he had been given a tracheotomy operation to enable him to breathe, so severe were his chest and lung injuries. Matt was not expected to live and a Catholic priest administered the last rites. It seemed that the 49-year-old Matt Busby was slipping out of this world. Only his own iron courage, and the sound physique he had built up in his days as a professional footballer, kept him going.

Johnny Berry lay silent in a deep coma. So, too, did the pilot Ken Rayment. Duncan Edwards had critical kidney injuries and his right thigh was smashed. A kidney machine was being flown to Munich from Stuttgart, in a desperate attempt to save his life.

That, in brief, was the medical opinion on the five most critically injured. No one, not even Maurer himself, could forecast who would live, but he and his team had scarcely stopped to get an hour's sleep as they strove to save the desperately ill.

As a survivor, I can confirm that those early hours after the crash were like a monstrous hangover. There were fleeting periods when I was quite conscious and almost euphoric; there were tangled moments of reality, and then a dream-like existence when I seemed to be floating, like a disembodied spirit. It was all so puzzling, like a jig-saw that wouldn't fit neatly into place.

No matter how hard I tried, my eyes didn't seem to focus properly. I kept looking at Matt Busby in the next bed, wondering what he was doing there.

I remembered leaving Belgrade, where I had had my own room in the Hotel Metropol. How come Busby was now in the same room? Why was Ken Rayment with us?

In brief periods of comprehension, I was also aware of the familiar faces of Press colleagues. Once, at the foot of my bed, I saw two good friends, Peter Lorenzo, then chief football writer of the *Daily Herald*, and Tony Stratton-Smith, a quite brilliant sports feature writer with the *Daily Sketch*. I couldn't quite make out why they should be standing there, looking so serious.

To break the silence, Peter started to talk to me about the Cup Draw for the World Cup in Sweden that year. He explained how England had been drawn in a tough section with Brazil and Russia, and we chatted quite amiably and coherently for several minutes; then, for some inexplicable reason, the faces of Lorenzo and Stratton-Smith began to fade. I blinked furiously to try and bring them back into focus. It was no use. I thought the lights had begun to fail and started to push myself up in bed. I couldn't manage it, I seemed to have no strength or will power, and without saying another word, I closed my eyes and fell deeply asleep.

This happened to me several times. I remember someone trying to pour some liquid down my mouth, from a vessel with a tiny spout, like a teapot. The liquid was not to my taste, so I opened my eyes and noticed for the first time a pretty young lady, with an angelic face and a large triangular sheet of white fastened in some way on her head.

'Let's have some beer, darling,' I shouted. The girl shook her head. 'Nein, Mr Taylor,' she said.

'I want beer,' I shouted back, 'or I'll be out of this bed to you.'

The girl smiled and wagged a reproving finger in my face like a school teacher admonishing a naughty schoolboy.

'I know what you mean,' she said. 'You shouldn't speak to me in that manner.'

I had no idea I was speaking to a nun, Sister Solemnis, who was to nurse me through the first dark hours of the tragedy. As she pushed that spout between my lips again, I spat it out and said to her, 'Come on, I want beer.'

A broadshouldered figure in white turned round from Matt Busby's bed and nodded to Sister Solemnis. 'It is all right, Sister. You can give him beer. He is a strong man.'

It was Maurer. I wondered what gave him the idea I was a strong man. I certainly didn't feel strong. All I wanted to do was sleep. And no sooner had Sister Solemnis given me a few drops of beer than my eyes started to close yet again.

This was crazy. First I thought I could sink a pint of beer, then I couldn't keep awake after a few drops.

When my eyes flickered and opened again, I thought I could see my brother Bill standing about two yards from my bed.

I opened my mouth to ask him what I was doing in this place. My lips formed the words, but no sound came from them, although I could hear his voice faintly, ever so faintly, as though coming from another world saying: 'Take it easy, Frank. You've got to rest.'

This crazy, mixed-up series of events had no continuity, no logicality; it was more like the product of a nightmare than of reality. I realised, in brief moments of clarity, that I was apparently lying on a bed somewhere, wearing a short white shirt, with my left arm and right leg encased in plaster. But I didn't seem to stay conscious long enough to ask where I was, why I was wearing a short white nightshirt or how I had managed to break an arm and a leg. Apart from that, I found breathing desperately painful. Worst of all, I couldn't fathom why I kept waking up with sudden, almost hilarious bursts of energy, only to feel my strength drain away almost immediately.

That Sunday night, when Busby and I were taken off the danger list, is still an evergreen memory. For the first time I came back to the reality of this world, and, after hovering on the brink of eternity, I was very very happy to be back.

If I close my eyes and concentrate, I can still recall the smell and the cool softness of the white sheets. Just for a second I thought I was in heaven, and then I smiled. What made me so sure I was going up there? No, I could feel the sheets, and it was so comforting. Even more comforting was the smiling face of my wife Peggy close to my bed. At first I had to squint very hard to make sure it was her, because I was still suffering blurring of vision.

She held my good right hand to reassure me.

'Where am I?' The words came faintly, although I was trying very hard to speak in my normal voice.

'In Munich. You have had a slight accident.'

'Did the kite (aeroplane) turn over?'

'Don't worry about what happened. You are safe and sound in Munich and that's all that matters.'

My mind was now quite clear, and as she mentioned the name Munich, I did a quick mental calculation and realised she must have come about 1,000 miles to be with me, although I knew Peggy didn't like travel as I did.

'I knew you would bloody well get here even if you had to walk,' I said cheekily, to emphasise what a wonderful person I knew she was.

'Ssh, be quiet,' she said. 'The doctors have told me you are going to be all right, if you obey instructions and keep quiet. You need a great deal of rest. Everything is all right at home and the boys send their love.'

My wife left the bedside to go to the open door to call my brother. 'He's awake now. You can come in.'

My eldest brother walked towards me, smiling, holding his hand out to shake hands. The last time I had seen Bill was three weeks previously, when I had been able to get tickets for him to join me in Workington for a Manchester United Cup tie.

'How are you feeling?'

'Pretty good. But I can't make out why I should feel so tired and weak. I keep falling asleep.'

'Don't worry about that. Lie back and take it easy. You're going to be all right.'

Slowly and methodically, I let my eyes wander curiously around the dimly lit room. I could see the figure of a man in the next bed with a kind of plastic tent around him. Was that really Matt Busby? I looked hard. Yes it was. So I hadn't been dreaming.

'That's Matt, isn't it? How is he doing?' I asked.

My wife replied, 'He's doing fine too. The doctors have just told Mrs Busby that he is going to get well. You are both going to be moved out of here. Now stop worrying. Everything is going to be all right.'

I didn't understand at that time, that we were in an intensive care unit, and that though Matt and I both had severe injuries, we were now considered well enough to be moved down the corridor into a normal hospital room.

As I lay there trying to piece things together, I realised I couldn't see any of my Press colleagues. Why weren't they in this room with me? When we travelled to European Cup ties we either shared a room or had one close by.

'Where's George Follows . . . Henry Rose, Eric Thompson and the rest of the lads?' I said.

This was the one question my wife and brother had been afraid I would ask. In my present weak state the shock of being told that they had been killed might be too much for me.

Peggy looked at me earnestly before saying, 'I am afraid they couldn't take them all here. They are safe in another place.'

Before I could pursue the matter further, I heard a voice I knew very well. It was Duncan Edwards, speaking very loudly and clearly.

'What time is the kick-off against Wolves on Saturday, Jim? I mustn't miss that match.' The question was directed at Jimmy Murphy, Manchester United's assistant manager.

I shall never forget that moment; many times over the years, when I have thought about it, I have felt like crying, because that question says all that anyone needs to know about Duncan Edwards. Here he was, lying virtually helpless and desperately injured, kept alive by a kidney machine, and yet all he could think about was playing football again for United.

I couldn't see the lump in Jimmy Murphy's throat, but I could hear it in his quick reply:

'We're resting you, Duncan,' he said. 'We don't need you to beat Wolves.' But Jimmy knew, even if we didn't, that Duncan Edwards would never play football again.

I watched Jimmy as he came over to speak to me. He was the same old Murphy – flashing eyes, big broad smile and the ready quip.

'How's big Duncan?' I asked.

'Fine . . . fine,' said Jimmy, who was also a particular friend of George Follows. He would know better than anyone where George and the rest of my Press friends were. I wanted my brother to meet Henry Rose, who had been my idol when I was a schoolboy, so I asked him, 'Jimmy, where are Henry, Eric, George and the rest of the lads? When they are well enough, I want you to take my brother to meet them. Where are they?'

Murphy had to think quickly. He didn't want to break the sad news to me at this stage, so up went his forefinger as though pointing to the floor above.

'They are all up there, son,' he said. 'Quite safe. They're in good hands, don't worry about that.' There was just a slight break in his voice, so he hastily changed the subject.

'You're a careless fellow,' he said, pointing to my right leg encased in plaster. 'Fancy giving your leg a knock like that. How's it feeling?' I didn't know what all the fuss was about my broken leg. I suffered no pain at all from either leg or my left arm, and I was quite content at that time to accept that they were both only minor fractures.

'I'm all right, Jimmy,' I replied. 'I'm fit enough to play on Saturday if selected.'

Jimmy Murphy liked nothing better than to joke with sports writers like George Follows and myself, by pointing out how unfit we were. This time he forced a smile: 'I know you will, son,' he said and walked away. He didn't speak to Matt Busby on that occasion, because Matt was sleeping, although as Jimmy left the room, he appeared to be brushing away a tear with his handkerchief.

By now I was beginning to understand that our airliner had crashed, although I was still trying to convince myself that we had just clattered through the perimeter fence. At times I was unable to accept the reality of the tragedy and tried to console myself with the thought that nothing had happened, that I was dreaming the whole strange episode, and that soon I would wake up to find myself rushing to catch the plane back from Belgrade to Manchester.

In those first 24 hours I could have died. So could Busby, Johnny Berry, and others too. For me, there would have been no real pain, apart from those brief moments in the ambulance before I was injected with morphia. Those who really suffered were the wives, mothers and sweethearts who flew from Manchester the morning after the accident, trying desperately to keep their spirits up, but living in an agony of dread. We, who lay so helpless and critically injured, could have fallen asleep and passed quietly away, without ever knowing; all our womenfolk could do was put on a brave face and live in hope, watching this life and death struggle taking place.

Perhaps only a woman could understand the torture of those hours – the feeling of nothingness, hope alternating with despair, realising that all they could do was wait, hope and pray, for the ultimate decision rested in other hands.

For two families – the Busbys and mine – prayers were answered on the Sunday night, some 72 hours after we had been taken to hospital. Professor Maurer was able to announce that Matt and I were off the critically ill list, although it was going to be a long, long time before either of us would be able to leave hospital. Perhaps it was fortunate we didn't realise how long and worrying that road to recovery would be; it was in fact a miracle we were still alive.

But there was no respite for Professor Maurer and his team. They were, to put it mildly, suffering extreme exhaustion from their efforts to keep a spark of life burning in the desperately ill, trying to save the lives of Johnny Berry, Duncan Edwards and Ken Rayment. Another patient now also needed constant care – Jackie Blanchflower, who at first had not been put alongside the most critically injured. In the intervening days there were ominous signs that he might have suffered the same severe kidney damage as Duncan Edwards.

I was playing a game with myself, because I didn't really want to think too deeply about what had happened. I instinctively realised, from my wartime experiences, that the person who frets and worries, allowing his mind to be dominated by depression, becomes a very morose patient and thereby slows down his own recovery. So I didn't want to think about the accident until I felt strong enough to work it all out in my mind. I was trying to convince myself that, like me, no one had suffered more than a few bruises and broken bones.

Nevertheless, there must be some reason why Matt, Duncan,

Johnny Berry and Ken Rayment were all in this area of the hospital together.

If I was being moved the following morning, what exactly was this room? When I put that question to my wife she replied:

'It's an operating theatre being used as an intensive care unit to treat people like Matt Busby and you.'

I had never previously been in an operating theatre in my life. I was, until then, the kind of person who felt quite illogically panic stricken at the very thought of going into an operating theatre. It used to make me feel sick and frightened.

'It is a good job I didn't know they had put me in an operating theatre,' I said grim faced. 'Otherwise I would probably have died from shock!'

I even managed to smile, a sure indication that I must be getting better. Even so, I hoped that I would not be seeing the inside of any more operating theatres.

My wife tucked me up in bed as though I were a baby. 'We've got to go now,' she said. 'Don't forget you are being moved into a proper room tomorrow morning, and the doctors have told us you are going to get better, and are off the danger list.'

Off the danger list? What on earth was Peggy talking about? I didn't know I had been on any danger list. Still it was a comforting thought. I didn't know then that anybody had been killed when Zulu Uniform crashed through the perimeter fence. I didn't know that the surgeons were still undecided whether it was going to be necessary to amputate my right leg or my left arm, or both.

Matt Busby was sleeping peacefully nearby. I fell asleep too.

Peggy, bless her, had come to Munich to look after me. My brother Bill was there as well. That was comforting.

I had no nightmares that night.

8   Room 401

The snow and sleet were still falling monotonously in Munich, and the skies were heavy and overcast as though weeping for those who had gone, when Matt Busby was wheeled out of the operating theatre on the Monday morning. He was now expected to live.

They wheeled Busby in a modern stainless-steel bed, so clean and so clinical, with its automatic back-rest. Down the corridor past the other operating theatres, grouped side by side; past the surgeons and theatre sisters in their white gowns and white masks and surgical boots preparing for another day's work; past the clusters of anaesthetic equipment.

At the far end of the corridor behind Busby's head was a giant board, like one of the huge boards one saw in a Fighter Command operations room during the war as they plotted the air battles. Only this board plotted the theatre list. On it were chalked the names of patients to be operated on that day, with the names of the surgeons alongside, which theatre they were using, and the times the operations were scheduled to start. Busby didn't notice these refinements of a modern hospital as they pushed him along. He had come safely along the grisly tightrope between life and death, but he was still in the no-man's-land between the world of the fully conscious and the world where people live and breathe, but where time and place has no meaning.

For some twenty-five yards he was wheeled down the corridor; through the frosted-glass doors, across the floor at the top of the stairs and through the plate-glass doors on the other side into Professor Maurer's private patients' section. First room on the left, Room 401, still near enough to the operating theatres and their equipment should aid be needed quickly. The large mahogany door opened easily with a touch, the handle large and cupped so that it could be opened with the slightest pressure of a nurse's elbow, should she have her hands full with medical equipment and want to get in quickly.

A spacious airy room with the walls in varied bright colours; not too vivid to strain the patient's eyes, but restful and still cheerful. There was ample room for two beds, a wash basin with concealed lighting in a recess, built-in wardrobes for two; on each bed a flexible reading light; the large light in the ceiling shielded to prevent the glare being thrown into a sick person's eyes and in the wall by each bed an oxygen cylinder.

Busby still needed oxygen to keep him going. In this room there was no need for the hospital staff to come trundling great unwieldy oxygen cylinders – it was there on tap, as you might have water and gas on tap.

On the further side of the room facing the door was a plastic shelf some three feet in width, large enough to take an array of flowers and pot plants, family photographs, bowls of fruit and a wireless set. The wall on this side was perhaps only 2 ft. 6 in. high. Above that nothing but plate glass for the entire length of the room. In the cosseted life of the hospital, a somewhat monastic unreal existence, the patient could still see the world outside; the clustered rooftops of Munich, the Bavarian State Parliament Building, and down the road the noble steeple of St John's Church; while four floors down in the roads outside there was the busy clatter of the trams, the honking of the cars, the hustle and bustle of people. Matt Busby and myself – for I was moved into that room along with him – were back among the living. But *only just*.

On the wall at the foot of the bed was a picture that radiated warmth and cheerfulness; a picture that made home feel not so far away: a picture of Her Majesty the Queen, Prince Philip and the then President of France, Mr Coty, on the occasion of the State Visit to France. That picture had been thoughtfully placed there by Her Majesty's Consul-General in Munich, Mr J. Somers Cocks. Its effect on the morale was magnificent.

There it hung for the twenty-one weeks I was to stay in Munich, and it was with regret I left it behind. It was quite startling to see how the Germans flocked round that picture, admiring our Queen. Their remarks were quite spontaneous as they spoke of Her Majesty. I had no idea that Germans felt that way about Royalty; that deep down many of them were still Royalists at heart, that they devoured every morsel and scrap of information about our Royal Family. Why? I was left with the impression that they were envious of our Royal heritage; of the stability it had given our country throughout the centuries; above all, that they admired the beauty and poise of the young woman who now sat on the British Throne. So I left that photograph of Her Majesty, which had been the centre of so much attention by the Germans who visited that room, as a memento to the nursing staff who looked after us so well.

Room 401 became a never-to-be-forgotten part of my life, for eighteen of the twenty-one weeks I was to stay in the Rechts der Isar Hospital were to be spent there.

On that first day I gazed long and intently at Matt Busby's inert form in bed, and at the plastic tent around his head. He did not speak; the nurses tip-toed quietly outside and I felt so terribly lonely. Anxiously I felt for the switch above my head to press the button and summon them back. A woman doctor came hurrying in and I tried to explain that I would like to speak to my mother in England. The doctor smiled understandingly, plugged in a telephone and within minutes I was speaking to England. I couldn't hold the receiver so the doctor held it for me; talking was difficult because breathing was painful. But I felt better as my seventy-eight-year-old mother spoke. 'I'm flying out to see you,' she said, 'when the doctors tell me I can come.' It was as though she were standing beside me in that room.

The phone was like a lifeline to a drowning man, bringing familiar voices. Newspapermen get sick to death of the incessant jangling of the phones in the office. It can be a godsend or a curse – depending how your story is going that day. At this time it was like heaven. I wanted to speak to my colleagues in the *News Chronicle* sports room in Manchester. As they came on I could hear the sweet music of the typewriters clack-clacking away, pounding out the stories; up there in the composing room the sub-editors would be sweating and cursing trying to shove the first edition through on time. Tom Simms was staggered by this unexpected call from his 'missing sports writer' unavoidably detained in Munich. Perkily he wisecracked: 'Now then, Frank, what about that soccer lead story you promised me for the North-East edition . . . time we had that.'

'Sorry, it's my day off,' I replied. 'I'm in bed having a rest.'

'All right, hope to see you soon, old pal,' replied the sports chief. I had done enough talking for one day. Once the receiver was down I fell asleep like Matt Busby.

In the dull grey of the following morning the snow was still drifting down, the roofs were covered with a white blanket and the huge Firestone Tyre advert on the wall of the big house opposite the hospital could scarcely be seen with the film of snow driven hard over it. The lovely sky-blue colour of the wall next to Busby's bed cheered and attracted my attention, much more than the chill sights outside. Sky blue, Manchester City's colours and not the flaming red of Manchester United. I shouted over to the United manager: 'Here I say, Matt, you can't stay here . . . look, City's colours.' At the time it seemed a funny remark. A grunt came from Matt Busby's bed; he was in great pain, not fully aware or even interested in his surroundings. He was too ill – and I was sorry I had spoken.

Matt was obviously in a bad way; the white-coated figures always seemed to be clustered round his bed doing something to his chest. Then he was wheeled outside and they said his broken foot had to be set without an anaesthetic. The thought made you wince. Busby never complained. He lay there silently, but for occasional bouts of coughing, when the tiny homely nun Sister Gilda would creep into the room and lean over him as a mother would a child in distress; a soothing figure trying to check and ease the pain which racked the man whenever he had a spasm of coughing.

After four days I was moved from Matt Busby's room, five doors down the corridor, to share a room with Jackie Blanchflower. Jack and I were in room 406 for three weeks, then we were moved together to room 401 – the room I had first shared with Busby. The doctors explained that Busby was in need of constant care and solitude. I think maybe I was talking too much for a man so desperately ill. So long as I was talking to someone I felt alive and alert, and Busby was in no state to talk to anyone. If I tried to read my eyes wouldn't focus properly after the first few sentences; conversation was the one way of passing the long daylight hours. It was a wrench to leave Busby behind, but everyone who came to his room was afraid that one slip of the tongue might reveal the full details of the tragedy to him. He was in no state to be told that just yet. And although I was in the same room as Busby I now knew a great deal of what had happened. How I found out I don't really know, except for some chance remark, and I turned fiercely on the German nurse sitting with me, shouting at her as though it were her fault: 'I have lost lots of pals in this accident, great chaps, Press colleagues – and now they are gone. I cannot think of them. I won't think of them. I daren't think of them or I would die too.'

She understood English, 'Sssh, you mustn't talk so . . . you must put such things from your mind . . . you are going to get well again.' So I tried to shut the faces of my friends out of my mind. When I thought of them, as I often did, I turned hastily to something else, something real that I could touch. But the whole grim sorrowful tragedy was gradually sinking in now and I was fearfully trying to hang on as I wept for those who had been killed. As the days passed I thought more and more of them. I could see them in the Press boxes joking, or writing or typing stories, bashing them away with wild glee.

That dreadful feeling of helplessness was worst of all. What could one say? What could one do? Here in Munich so many many miles away from Manchester – here in a hospital bed scarcely able to move?

There were the times, too, when it still seemed like some fearful nightmare, that one day the sun would come shining through and they would all be there and and I would wake up. Through the windows you could see the snow still falling. It wasn't a dream, it was so devastatingly, undeniably true after all.

I felt so heart-breakingly sorry for all these young footballers, young men who were so fit, lost like that in a matter of seconds. Most of all, I thought of my Press colleagues, for I had known them all so long and knew most of their wives and families. The public knew them chiefly as a by-line in their favourite paper, but I knew them as men, rivals – deadly rivals in the exacting business of chasing sports news. But they were part of the Brotherhood of the Press who lived and eventually died for their craft.

Henry Rose, Don Davies and Alf Clarke had lived through the fury of two wars; George Follows, Tom Jackson, Eric Thompson, Archie Ledbrooke and Frank Swift were in the battle line during the Second World War, and now they had died like this.

'O God, help their families in their hour of need . . . O God, give me strength.'

9 The Leg and I

Jackie Blanchflower was once the most exciting centre-half in English football. Now he weighs 17 stone and occasionally goes to watch Manchester United play, but deep down Jackie knows, as I know, that he was one of the tragic casualties of the Munich Air Crash.

I find it sad that when one mentions the name of Blanchflower, soccer fans automatically think of Danny, captain of the glorious Spurs team (which became the first club to win the double of League Championship and FA Cup this century) and so few people remember his younger brother Jackie.

As the younger brother, Jackie always had a great deal to live up to. Danny was the one with the style, elegance and silver tongue. Jackie was at first rather the odd-job man. It is true that he had enough ability to catch the eyes of the Manchester United talent spotters, so he went to Old Trafford as an inside forward. In another club, he might have made that position his own. At Old Trafford, he wasn't good enough to keep out the likes of Dennis Viollet, Bobby Charlton and Bill Whelan. So Jackie, inevitably, was moved to wing half, where it was hoped his lack of speed might not be so noticeable.

Some hope. At that time, Matt Busby had an abundance of wing half-backs which included Duncan Edwards, Eddie Colman, Jeff Whitefoot, Don Gibson and Freddie Goodwin, plus two youngsters by the name of Wilf McGuinness and Nobby Stiles.

I feel it is necessary to mention these facts, to illustrate the difficulties Jackie Blanchflower had simply to earn a regular place in the Manchester United first team. Nothing seemed more certain than that he would end his days as an honest journeyman, but never a star like Danny.

Then he had his lucky break. He was picked to play centre-half for his country, Northern Ireland, where his style was a revelation. He had always had skill, but now he had more time to use that skill and the ability to read the game and control the defence, as Bobby Moore was to do so brilliantly for England some years later.

In a few months, Jackie Blanchflower's style at centre-half had caught the imagination of the soccer experts who for years had raged against the dull defensive styles of the stopper centre-half. Instead of trying to cripple opponents with lunging tackles, Jackie was much more intelligent, taking the ball by clever interceptions, and once he had the ball at his feet, he was able to use it constructively. In a nutshell, as a centre-half he had style, and there were many sports writers – myself included – who felt that at long last, Jackie had found his true position, and that it was only a question of time before he would be rivalling brother Danny as one of the big personalities in the game.

Jackie was looking forward to an exciting future, and especially to playing in the 1958 World Cup in Sweden. Munich was to change all of that. The Jackie Blanchflower who shared a room with me in the Rechts der Isar hospital was only a shadow of the smiling, wisecracking Jackie I had known previously. I realised then, when I could see the agony, despair and shock of the Air Crash etched on his once carefree face, that he would never play first-class football again. When we started that last fatal attempt to take off, Jackie was a footballer with a potentially great career ahead of him. In the crash his right arm was fractured, and even now, it still gives him pain. His pelvis was also fractured, and the most worrying injury of all was the damage to his kidneys, which fortunately did not prove as dangerous as at first expected.

Nevertheless, those injuries robbed football of the burgeoning talents of Jackie Blanchflower, a man who could have done so much to halt the decline into the boring blocking tactics which disfigure the game today. Whatever faults he had as a footballer, I do not think anyone could have changed Jackie Blanchflower into an automaton.

As I was then 37 years old, I had no worries about trying to get myself built up again into a fit athlete. My athletic days had finished 12 years previously, when I re-started my career as a journalist at the end of World War II.

With Jackie Blanchflower, Bobby Charlton, Bill Foulkes,

Dennis Viollet, Ray Wood, Ken Morgans and Albert Scanlon it was far different. As professional footballers they must have been scared stiff that their injuries might cut short their career and their livelihood.

So, as Jackie lay brooding in the bed next to mine, I tried to console myself that, no matter what had happened, the only thing that mattered for me was to get back on two legs, and carry on with my career as a sports writer. In that sense I was lucky.

Day after day, sometimes three times a day, we were visited by a jolly, stockily built man wearing a doctor's white coat. By now his face was very familiar, because I recognised him as the man who had told the nun I could have a drink of beer. He fascinated me by the way he came striding into the room, very purposefully like a sergeant-major. In everything he did, he radiated authority and confidence.

I didn't know his name, and I was almost afraid to ask. Finally I managed to whisper in my wife's ear while he was attending to Jackie Blanchflower:

'Who is this fellow? Everybody jumps to it when he speaks.'

'It is Professor Maurer,' my wife whispered. 'He is the chief surgeon.' This was the first time I heard the name of the man to whom we all owed our lives. A name none of us will ever forget.

Through all these years I have been able to picture him, just as he was then. His very presence was like a shaft of hope and sunlight in our sick room.

Maurer had more than a touch of the showman about him. He would come bustling in to see his patients, with beaming alert eyes, never failing to give a quick and courteous bow should there be any visitors in the room. Maurer didn't seem to mind his patients having visitors, and that made a pleasant change from the iron discipline of some British hospitals at that time. Maurer's philosophy was, 'A happy patient is a good patient, and easier to look after.'

He realised that Jackie was brooding; so, although he had few words of English, he quickly started to call Blanchflower by his first name. 'Now zen, Jackie, wie geht es Ihnen?' Very quickly Maurer broke through the barriers of language with his cheerful chuckle and the concentrated care he gave to each of his patients.

When he came to my bed, he would whisk back the

bedclothes and closely examine my right leg which had a huge plaster around it, and some kind of cage embedded in it. He would enquire whether I had any pains from my broken ribs and collar bone, and whether my suppurating left arm hurt. To be perfectly honest, I didn't suffer any severe pains until one night, when apparently the plaster had trapped the sciatic nerve. Because I had once been an even-time sprinter, I had always taken good care of my legs when I played soccer or rugby. To put it bluntly, I was dead scared of ever breaking a leg. Each day he visited me, Professor Maurer called for a stainless steel trolley to be wheeled in, with an array of scalpels, forceps and other surgical instruments. I could see him busy with probes and forceps, apparently fishing out bits of metal and dirt, nodding and smiling as he performed this work. I knew what he was doing, but apart from an occasional dull ache, it didn't really hurt.

This surprised me, because I had always been one of nature's cowards. For example, the week before this accident, I had been travelling to a Cup tie with Joe Hulme, the former Arsenal and England right winger. On the way to this match at Goodison Park between Everton and Blackburn Rovers, Joe was talking about a recent accident in which Alick Jeffrey, an outstanding young footballer, had had his leg broken playing for England Under 23 against France.

As an old professional, Joe capped that story by referring to an accident in his playing days, when a player tried to stand up after a tackle and the broken bone came through his stocking.

That story made me cringe. I could feel the pain, like anybody else would. Yet here I was, a week later, with a very badly smashed right leg, and it was nowhere near as painful as I had imagined it would be.

As Professor Maurer bent over my leg I would try to see exactly what was wrong, but, happily, I never was able to see just how badly mangled my leg was, otherwise I would no doubt have fretted and delayed my eventual recovery.

Within a few days, though, I had a very disturbing shock. Maurer and his assistants were clustered around the foot of my bed, and I just caught one word of what they were saying: INFECTION.

A chill fear gripped me. Did this mean an infection was

spreading up my right leg, and that it would have to be amputated? Oh God, no!

Yet, no matter how hard I tried, I could not dismiss that fear. The name of Derek Dooley flashed into my mind. In the early 1950s, spectators laughed at first when Sheffield Wednesday introduced into their team a tall, rangy ginger-haired centre-forward named Derek Dooley. A six-footer, with carroty-coloured hair and wearing size 12 soccer boots, Derek was ready-made for slick headline writers, who quickly dubbed him the Scorer in Seven League Boots.

Dooley didn't mind. He knew he was no stylist, but he chased and chased all over the field, harrying defenders, often clumsily, and he was a sensational goal scorer. He managed to put the ball in the net off his knees, ankles or shoulders, and scored other goals with snorting headers and shots.

Dooley the Brave shot his team into the First Division in his first season, and in so doing broke the Sheffield Wednesday goal scoring record. Once in the First Division, he took time to settle down and a few critics thought that Dooley had had one lucky season, and that that would be the end of him. In fact Dooley came back to emerge as a terror to centre-halves in the First Division. Crowds everywhere flocked to see this ungainly goal scoring genius who seemed to have no ball control, no great footballing brain, and yet was proving an unstoppable match winner. Despite his lack of finesse, he was strongly tipped to be England's next centre forward, until he fell in a collision with a goalkeeper, when Sheffield Wednesday played Preston North End at Deepdale.

Dooley was taken to hospital with what appeared to be an uncomplicated broken leg; four days later, a nurse saw tell-tale signs on Dooley's plastered leg. Hastily specialists were called, and confirmed that he had gas gangrene. Their advice was terse and to the point: Dooley either lost his leg or his life. There was no other way.

A tiny cut on the back of his ankle was blamed as the source of infection. Thus Derek Dooley's short but thrilling football career ended under the surgeon's knife – a heart-rending tragedy made more bearable by Dooley's matchless courage as he cheerfully smiled at the surgeon.

'OK, Doc. If it's got to come off, let's get it over with.'

Can you blame me recalling that tragedy as I lay helpless in hospital? If Dooley had got gas gangrene from a tiny cut, how much greater was the chance that I had picked up that infection from the dirt and slush around the wreckage of the aircraft.

I was gripped by a freezing fear that it *had* happened to me. I tried to shut the Dooley tragedy out of my mind – only to find a substitute. I started thinking instead about that First War film *All Quiet on the Western Front*, when a German soldier comes back from the operating theatre and tries to wiggle his toes. When he doesn't see any movement under the bedclothes he lifts them to take a look . . . and the dreadful truth dawns on him that his leg isn't there any more.

I spent hours absolutely petrified. I was of course completely selfish in worrying like this, when Maurer's team were still fighting desperately to save the lives of Duncan Edwards, Ken Rayment and Johnny Berry.

Eventually, after a sleepless night, my wife turned up as usual in the morning to see me and I blurted out to her, 'I know the truth about my leg, Peggy. It is infected. It might be gangrene like Derek Dooley had, and they had to amputate his leg. Don't let them do that to me . . . please . . . ask if I have got gangrene. I am not going to let those Germans wheel me out of this room and then take my leg off without knowing about it . . .'

My wife had suffered more than enough already, but she did not show it, not even by the flicker of an eyelid or a trembling lip. She looked me straight in the eyes:

'Aren't you forgetting your friends . . . George Follows, Henry Rose and Eric Thompson? What about them? They are not here to complain. You ought to realise how thankful we all are that you are alive. Both your leg and your arm are infected, but it is not gangrene. The doctors have assured me of that. You ought to thank God you are not maimed or blinded.'

At first I couldn't believe this was my own wife speaking to me in this way. Yet how right she was. How easy it would have been for her to utter words of glib sympathy, and then no doubt we would both have dissolved in tears. There were to be many more times, while I was in hospital, where I found that in general, women can face up to these crises far better than men. They may wilt and cry for what seems to men the most illogical reasons, but when common sense and courage are needed, they often display a backbone of steel. That is the way it was with my wife. She wasn't going to let me quit . . . not even if I came out of hospital on one leg.

As she turned away for a moment, I surreptitiously poked my fingers in my eyes, to feel they were still there. I had to convince myself I could see, and that I was not imagining this scene. Suddenly I felt ashamed. I realised all that Peggy had said to me was a realistic view of my present condition, but I wasn't going to let her get away with it.

As she tucked me more firmly into my bed, I said very tartly, 'It is all very well you talking like that, but it isn't your leg. You ought to know I used to be a very good sprinter. All my life I've tried to be fit and to get about without relying on other people. This is Germany, not England. How do I know whether they might just take my leg off without warning me? I don't want to end up as a cripple.'

Such an idea was of course laughable, but at that moment I was so upset I was practically shouting at my wife.

She didn't raise her voice, but spoke to me very quietly and firmly:

'Don't be so ridiculous,' she said. 'You ought to realise that after all the care and attention you have received from the doctors and nurses in this hospital, there is not the slightest chance they would do such a thing. They are keeping me informed, and I see no reason to doubt them.' Peggy stopped momentarily and smiled. 'In any case, you don't type with your feet, do you?'

That humorous remark did the trick. Even I laughed as I replied, 'You had better tell that to Tom Simms and all the sub editors on the *News Chronicle*. They reckon my typing is so bad that only someone who used his feet instead of his hands could make so many mistakes.'

I felt a little bit more confident after that. Peggy, however, was determined to make me realise that I needed to show more guts if I was ever going to overcome my present problems.

'Whenever you feel depressed,' she said, 'just remember Douglas Bader and how he overcame his handicap.'

I knew all about Bader, because my brother Don had played cricket against him in the RAF while I was still a schoolboy.

Don had told me all about this marvellously gifted sportsman who had lost both legs in an air crash and refused to accept defeat, often turning cartwheels in the hospital wards to keep the other patients amused.

His exploits as the legless Battle of Britain pilot gave Bader world-wide renown and, as a newspaperman, I had seen many photographs of Bader, laughing and joking as he stumped around the hospital wards on his tin legs, encouraging others – especially children who had suffered limb damage – to emulate his example.

Once again, by mentioning Bader, my wife had struck the right note. Compared with him, my problem was a minor one. Yet that struggle to save a leg – my leg – was a very personal one. In my black moments I used to think that if they amputated my leg I would die. At other times I would encourage myself by saying, 'If Dooley and Bader can overcome this kind of problem, so can I.' Alas we haven't all got that kind of spirit. As I fell asleep that night I muttered into my pillow, 'Bader? Yes, he could do it, but Bader had guts!'

Bader remained one of my heroes. When I eventually met him at a meeting of the Central Council of Physical Recreation, I told him how his example had helped me.

'That's very kind of you, old boy,' he said. 'You know, if you lose an arm they can give you a hook. And if you lose a leg they can give you tin legs and then you never get your feet wet. The people I admire are the paraplegics. The guts they display when playing basketball is really unbelievable. They are cracking people.'

Unfortunately Bader was not with me in Munich to inspire me then, but my wife made a pretty good substitute.

Sympathy there was in plenty for the injured men after the accident; for weeks afterwards, the newspapers carried stories about the resolute courage of the survivors. Perhaps in some cases that was true, but the longer I stayed in hospital, the more I became convinced we had all got it wrong. The courageous ones were the womenfolk, who lived in the shadow of fear for days and even weeks – like Johnny Berry's mother and his wife, who waited and hoped for over five weeks while he lay unconscious, before he finally cheated death.

Then there was Jean Busby and her daughter Sheena,

constantly at Matt's bedside to give him the support and strength he needed to survive.

Probably the bravest of all was Mrs Rayment who, because her husband Ken was a pilot, must obviously have worried for years that he might one day be involved in an air crash. A pilot's wife accepts that risk when she marries him, but it does not make it any easier when her fear becomes a reality.

Mrs Rayment spent hour after hour by her husband's bedside, often shouting into his ear: 'Come on Ken . . . Time to get up.' She kept using normal words and sentences about his job and the family in the hope it would break through the coma. I can guess now what she was going through, but in the few weeks I knew her, she never let it show. She hid her sorrow under a warm and lovely smile, whenever she came into my room to see Peggy and enquire how I was getting on.

I remember joking with her about the last night in Belgrade, saying, 'I owe Ken a drink, you know. He bought the last one in Belgrade.'

She smiled gaily. 'I'll remind him of that when he wakes up.'

It is another of the tragedies of the Munich Air Crash that he never did wake up. Ken Rayment's last words before he fell into that fatal coma were: 'Are my passengers all right?'

That is how I shall always remember him. Just as I shall always remember the stoical courage of some of the wives, mothers and sweethearts who arrived in Munich to nurse their loved ones. They were just ordinary people, thrust by an accident into a blazing spotlight of publicity.

Munich left its mark on me too, leaving me with a streak of pragmatism I had never previously possessed.

For some years I had enjoyed the prestige and personal publicity of a big by-line in the newspaper. Now it no longer had any importance. Just to be able to walk again and have my health was much more important.

When the newspapers arrived from England, I would read with a wry smile stories about some busty film starlet who was reported as saying after marrying for the third time: 'Gosh . . . this is for real this time . . .' Who cares about such things? It is the simple, human values of ordinary people that matter. From the day I was married I had never really given any serious thought to my marriage vows . . . 'In sickness and in health.'

Now all around me, I could see how so many of the wives of the survivors were true to those vows.

My wife used to smile tolerantly when I cut myself; she knew better than anybody that I was never a natural hero at the sight of blood, especially my own blood. Now I was really in a bloody mess. So when Professor Maurer probed into my flesh, my wife would stand on the right side of my bed to hold my hand.

Every few seconds, while the Professor was cleaning out the wounds, he would stop and ask, 'You have pains, Mr Taylor?'

I would shake my head and reply, 'No sharp pain, Professor. Just a dull kind of ache, but I can stand that.'

'He must be too thick in the head to feel anything, Professor Maurer,' my wife would say, although I could tell from the way she tensed and the sudden way she gripped my hand tightly, that she was suffering the pain for me.

That's the way I saw it with all these wonderful women who hastened to the side of the injured in Munich. The small talk; the hours of forced conversation, when their hearts must have been close to breaking point; the hours when they were closeted together in the Stacchus Hotel, trying to think of anything, talk of anything but the accident and their loved ones lying in the hospital just up the hill.

The weaker sex? As I said, Munich turned me into a pragmatist, so I know that many of these women (our women) were the bravest of the brave. Without them, many more would have died!

10   Angels of Munich

Day followed day, inevitably, inexorably, painstakingly, like a film in slow motion. And always it was snowing. Did it ever do anything else in Munich? At six o'clock in the morning or soon after the door would open quietly and into the room would glide Sister Solemnis. Slender and youthful, that great triangular white cap on her head like a jib sail on a racing yacht. It looked so cumbersome; and yet she wore it with dignity above a serene face that would have been described as beautiful had she employed the cosmetic artifices of the world outside.

She would arrive with such a gentle smile that, unknown to her, I went hot and cold as I recalled the boisterous way I had shouted and raved at her when I first came round in the operating theatre. This was the girl who had sat by my bedside hour after hour administering oxygen – kind, resourceful, patiently nursing this unknown Britisher back to life. And now she had to deal with me as though I were a babe in arms – and a rather portly babe at that!

'Good morning, Mr Taylor. Did you sleep well? Any pains during the night? Are you feeling better today?' She spoke English easily, almost faultlessly, without a trace of any harsh guttural German accent. She had been brought up from her earliest years by nuns; and now she had dedicated her life to being a nun herself. From six in the morning till eight o'clock at night she worked, with time off to attend medical studies but no days off from the hospital, devoted to her faith and the patients she nursed. A young life of great self-denial from someone who saw more to life than killing the hours in an Espresso bar listening to rock-'n'-roll records from a juke-box. Not the sort of life many could undertake, perhaps, but the serenity and sense of happy dedication was there for all to see. This young nun was working directly under Sister Gilda, who had herself been for more than twenty-five years in the Rechts der Isar.

They were just two of the people soon to be known to the outside world as the 'Angels of Munich'. They were certainly two of the most unforgettable characters one could meet on a lifetime's journey.

The delicate hands of Sister Solemnis quickly took the eye – long, well formed and supple as a concert pianist's . . . and they were so gentle.

She would come to the bedside with a bowl of water and gently, ever so gently, bathe my face, then my left arm (the one free from plaster), then my chest and leg. It was as though she were handling a baby. At first she even had to clean my teeth for me.

In his room Busby had to be washed in the same way. Blanchflower could manage some of these tasks himself.

In the early hours of the night sleep always seemed to elude Jack, as he clung feverishly to consciousness. At last he would fall into a deep sleep and, because it was what his troubled mind needed, the nuns would leave him there, long past normal waking hours, until at 7.30 the door would open again and in would come Sister Solemnis or Sister Gilda saying softly: 'Come on, Jackie. Wakey, wakey, Jackie. Breakfast.' I don't know where they picked up that Service phrase 'Wakey, wakey' but it sounded extraordinarily funny when said by the Germans. Only with difficulty at first was Jackie able to feed himself and Sister Solemnis had to spoon mine to me – two lightly boiled eggs, shelled and put in a tumbler. She pushed the food into my mouth in tiny helpings, while I, propped up in bed, fumed at this helplessness. Her manner soon made me realise that there was nothing else for it but to put up with such feeding with as good a grace as possible. After all, there were more important and interesting things to do in a hospital than feeding a patient! The tea, either with lemon or peppermint, was dribbled into my mouth with that infuriating invalid cup. At the end of two weeks I was allowed some small rashers of bacon, thinly cut. I might have a few broken bones and my body was a trifle battered, but no one could say there was anything wrong with my digestion or appetite. Not so Jack Blanchflower. He ate but little, despite the Sisters' gentle persuasion.

'Eat, Jackie . . . come on. It is good for your arm. Eat and you will get well.' Most of these nurses were nuns, but they laughed and teased just as English nurses do. Jackie celebrated his twenty-fifth birthday in the hospital and when the great day dawned he was, as usual, fast asleep.

Into the room crept Sister Gilda and Sister Solemnis with a gigantic birthday cake which they had ordered from the hospital bakery. They placed it, a magnificent creation, on a gaily decorated table as the German nurses and orderlies gathered in a circle singing and giggling: 'Happy Birthday to you. Happy Birthday to you. Happy Birthday, dear Jackie, Happy Birthday to you.'

Outside the world looked dull and overcast but inside that room all was cheerful, merry and bright as Jackie sleepily woke up rubbing his eyes and then bursting with smiles as he caught sight of the scene. 'Thank you . . . thank you.' He really didn't know quite what to say.

With such thoughtful attention, the cheerful nurses, the doctors as they padded in and out and the constant flow of visitors, the days passed not too badly. At eight o'clock at night Sister Solemnis would come in for the last time. Although I am not a Catholic, she would sprinkle the Holy Water. She would ask yet again: 'Have you any pains, are you all right, is there anything else I can do for you?' And then she would slip out of the door as silently as she had entered it in the morning, pausing just long enough to whisper: 'I will pray for you both.' And she was gone.

When you are clinging to life as we were then, how inconsequential seem the religious arguments about dogma. High Church . . . Low Church . . . Catholic . . . Protestant . . . Presbyterian . . . Methodist . . . Salvation Army. It is surely one army of Christians. Why? The road to heaven is broad enough to take them all!

The last caller of the day was always Sister Gilda. Short, almost dumpy, so very tiny and very precise in her movements . . . like a mother coming round to see all her children safe in bed. First to Jackie to see that he was warm enough in this wintry weather, to ask whether his broken arm troubled him, to see whether he would be able to sleep without a drug. Then to my side of the room, to see whether the stainless-steel rail which prevented me falling out of bed was securely in position, to ask whether I was in pain and needed a sleeping draught. A touch on the toes of my right foot to make sure they were not cold or whether there were any tell-tale signs of worse trouble developing beneath the plaster. A warm steady smile, a firm handclasp. *'Gute Nacht. Schlafen Sie gut'* [Good night. Sleep well], and then she, too, was gone to evening prayers and to bed between nine-thirty and ten, for she had to be up between four-thirty and five in the morning to go into the little church in the hospital. At 6 am she was back among her patients on Station 1. Thus the days rolled along. We were cushioned from the harsh world outside, from the necessity and worry of making any decisions, carefully comforted and cosseted as life buzzed busily and peacefully with nurses and hospital staff in constant attendance. The nights were not so comforting, alone with one's thoughts. The accident which I had first imagined as a little mishap with the plane overshooting the runway, was now quite clearly a bloody and fearsome tragedy. Easy in the daytime to push into the background the sorrow which welled up inside you. At night-time the images kept coming back . . . coming back.

Oh God, why had I been spared when they had not? I was grateful . . . but why? . . . why? How were their families getting along? How could I face them when I got back to England? What could I tell them? What comfort could I bring? The questions kept pressing forward and there were no answers.

It sounded so silly and so trite: 'I was just sitting there quite OK when I got a clump behind the ear and woke up in hospital.'

How could I explain just why it was, for the first and only time on these flights, I had sat alone and been saved, while they had sat laughing and leg-pulling in the tail of the machine and been killed?

What Protecting Hand had reached out and shielded me?

Why me? Why not them? The tormenting thoughts kept trickling into the brain. That scene in the operating theatre when I had asked for Henry Rose, and Jimmy Murphy with lightning inspiration pointed quickly upwards. Now I knew what he meant when he said: 'Henry is safe up there.' Henry, the swashbuckling, breezy, bouncing Henry Rose, a great showman who had these thirty years and more been a kingpin in Northern Sport . . . GONE. Sports editor, chief Northern sports writer for the *Daily Express*, the chap who had the fans chanting for him whenever he appeared at the Liverpool grounds, Goodison Park or Anfield. Never again would that thick portly figure with the brown trilby hat, the inevitable cigar clamped between his teeth, make the grand entrance of the Press boxes on the soccer grounds.

There never was a slicker storyteller, and many of those stories were told against his own Jewish race. The quick twinkle of those brown eyes as he said: 'I never bothered to get married. I was married to my job on the *Daily Express* thirty years ago.'

Unlike the public's mistaken idea of hard-drinking, harum-scarum sports writers, Henry did not drink. He would stand at a bar and take a tonic water or a lemonade while the beer-swillers milled round him. When he wasn't bustling round the *Express* sports desk, he spent the midnight hours playing poker, often with Maurice Winnick, famed orchestra leader and now television impresario, who had been a friend of Henry's for years.

Churning out columns of sports news was Henry's life; now he had died for it. Henry who used to proclaim: 'I'll keep on sports writing till I don't find it fun any more. But the public soon forget. Bet you within three weeks of my retirement the soccer fans will be saying: "Henry Rose? Who's Henry Rose? Never heard of him. Who did he play for?"'

Henry, old pal, you are wrong. The 'Whackers' of Merseyside who used to howl for your blood, and the other football fans too, can never forget you any more than I can. How could they? For the football followers roared in disgust or laughed with joy at the man who made so many daft forecasts. As a writer Henry was never the best of that sports-writing circle in Manchester. As a stylist and coiner of unforgettable phrases George Follows reigned supreme. For knowledge and appreciation of the finer points of the game Archie Ledbrooke, Don Davies and Frank Swift couldn't be bettered. For wit Eric Thompson was No. 1. And for the inside news of what was happening at Old Trafford the Manchester evening-paper men Tom Jackson and Alf Clarke knew it all. But Henry was the great showman, the chap who quickly realised what the man in the street was talking about and wrote accordingly; who used to boom: 'I'm not interested in the smart phrase, or the perfect prose style. I just wanna know what the man in the four-ale bar thinks of the *Daily Express* and Henry Rose. That's who I write for and try to entertain.'

So he wrote fantastically, at times infuriatingly. Like the time he blandly announced that he was quite sure the famous Arsenal football team would not lose another match with six weeks of the season still remaining. It was the sort of forecast that would make any football manager reach for the aspirin bottle muttering: 'Oh no . . . preserve us from this.' Sure enough, the very day the article appeared, Henry went to Blackpool to see them beat Arsenal. At one point he thought he might need a police escort to get him away from the crowd. They sent him rude telegrams; sticking-plaster to seal his lips; suggestions that he should start writing comic scripts for the Goons instead of writing about soccer; stinking fish for his supper.

Henry loved every moment of the controversies he so readily started. He stood on his pulpit and let the *Express* readers hurl their brickbats and their occasional bouquets at him. Some said he was a Big Head, this oh so flashy sports writer of the *Express*. Yet in the time I knew him I never found him guilty of an underhand deed on a fellow journalist.

If anything, he leaned over backwards to help the beginner at the trade. Like that time in Bilbao. Manchester United had lost a European Cup match 5–3 in a blinding snowstorm and there were Henry and myself sharing a room, anxiously counting the minutes waiting for the telephone lines to be cleared so that we could send our stories.

No calls came. Just a long and ominous silence. I went downstairs to find out from the girl on the switchboard what had happened. The dark-haired, lustrous-eyed señorita tried to explain there were only six lines and it was most difficult to get telephone calls through from England to Bilbao. I thanked her; told her I was going into the lounge next to the switchboard for a sherry and if any calls came for Mr Rose or myself I was to be told *immediatement*, not to mention *toute de suite*. She understood I must be told quickly. I had scarcely finished ordering a glass of sherry when the *Mirror* man Archie Ledbrooke came gasping through the door like Roger Bannister finishing a sub-four-minute mile. 'Quick, Frank . . . the *News Chronicle* is on the phone for you . . . and they are rationing the time to six minutes a call.' I hurtled out of the room, taking the stairs two at a time, saying a few choice words about the Spanish señorita on the switchboard in my headlong flight. As I raced into our room, there was Henry Rose puffing away at a cigar, sitting wrapped up in a vast dressing-gown sending over the first part of my typewritten story to the *News Chronicle* sports desk.

I took over and sent about a third of my piece over when the switch cut us off. 'Sorry, we ring again later.'

I turned sheepishly to Henry to thank him for sending over the opening paragraphs. He wagged an admonitory finger. 'Taylor, as a young journalist you should know, get the story over first . . . you eat, drink and sleep afterwards.' Annoyed, I tried to explain that I was in fact sitting next to the switch and if there was any nearer place than that, would he mind telling me. Furthermore, that if the señorita couldn't shout four or five yards to tell me my call was on, then it was a pretty poor affair. Henry grinned. 'All right, I'll accept that.'

The phone arrangements between Bilbao and Manchester that night were as crazy as a Marx Brothers film; we were all cut off so often that one would think we were sending some highly critical political commentary which needed to be censored, instead of a report of a football match. After being cut off several times, Henry disappeared from the room, being told that it would be a further hour before he could speak to the *Express* again. In a matter of minutes the sports desk of the *Express* were on; there was nothing for it but for me to start pushing over some of Henry's copy until the page boy found him. I heard the pitter-patter of heavy feet in the corridor, and Henry appeared, cigar clamped angrily between his teeth, a huge bath towel draped round his middle, a pool of water collecting where he stood. 'Give me that phone.' He dictated the rest of his story shivering like some Roman senator disturbed during his bath night.

I chortled as he finished: 'Next time, Rose, you might send your story before you take a bath.'

He beamed broadly and disappeared down the corridor to finish his plunge. In seconds he was back again with that towel still ridiculously draped round his middle like a toga and he ceremoniously handed me the butt end of a cigar. 'Here you are, Frank,' he said, 'don't say I never give you anything.' And he left me there looking rather foolish, holding a tattered piece of cigar.

That dizzy señorita on the switchboard kept intoning with maddening frequency: 'There are many hours' delay on the calls from England.' I don't think she had ever had to cope with a squad of Pressmen rushing against the clock to get their stories back to England to catch the editions. I was the unlucky one, for it was close to midnight when I was able to send over the last three paragraphs to complete my chore for the day. The banquet was over; the officials of Manchester United and Bilbao had delivered their speeches on the friendships welded through sport. The tables were cleared and most of the players and officials had left as I finished my call.

Henry Rose grabbed me and piloted me to the top table, bare save for one place neatly laid out. Summoning the head waiter he said: 'This is the friend I was telling you about. He has not eaten since midday. Do you think you can give him his meal now?'

That's the way it was with the Manchester Press gang. They would scoop you at the drop of a hat on any story; outside of that, they were the happiest, most considerate of companions. In the night-time gloom in Munich, how could I shut out the memories of these unforgettable characters? Time and time again I was back with them in the Press boxes of England's soccer grounds or on those trips across the continent in the European Cup.

Remember Prague? That was just six short weeks ago. When Manchester United drew with Dukla in Prague's Red Army Stadium; when they wouldn't let you phone from your bedroom, but insisted that all calls must be made from the box in the hall. Remember? That was the time we had all that fun with Don Davies.

In his lifetime millions of radio listeners came to love the voice of Don Davies. Every Saturday lunchtime he was on the air with his friends and BBC colleagues, Eamonn Andrews, Charlie Buchan, Charles Harrold and the two Alans in Manchester, Alan Clarke and Alan Dixon. That was his pre-match radio chat, as the soccer fans all over the country were having lunch before going to watch their favourite team play. At 5.30 he would be back on the air again, on the Angus McKay

Sports Report programme, with that droll Lancashire voice turning out the jewelled phrases with the ease of a housewife shelling peas.

There was the time when he warned the housewives of Manchester with due solemnity: 'Now then, ladies, if your hubby is a little restless today, if he cannot eat that fine lunch you've cooked for him, be patient with him. You see, he wants to get off to watch Manchester City play Manchester United and he'll get enough meat and drink from the incidents in this game to chew over all week with his mates.'

The 1955 Cup Final at Wembley, when Don Davies gazed transfixed as Manchester City came out of the players' tunnel wearing vivid eye-blinding blue track suits; as Newcastle United marched alongside them in their normal, practical black-and-white-striped playing kit. Don captured the scene in one vivid phrase. 'Well,' he says, 'this is obviously going to be a battle between the Gaudies and the Geordies.'

In the tumult and shouting at Windsor Park, Belfast, Don Davies, from his eyrie in the Press box, looked on in mild astonishment as the Irish centre-forward that day chased and thundered about the field like a wild buffalo harassing England's Billy Wright. 'Hey, dearie me,' said Don as he watched this strange creature unleashed for an unsuspecting international occasion, 'he strikes me like a fellow who has been serving behind the bar all morning in a green baize apron, called time and told the customers: "Sorry boys, but Oi've to lead the Irish forward line against England now."' Davies was right, this chap looked like a man who should have been kicking unwanted customers out of a bar, instead of kicking a ball in an international match.

That's how this lovable little man Don Davies wrote and talked about the game of football; the scintillating phrase, the cloth cap, the homely witticisms, it all added up to a remarkable character who in his time had played soccer as an amateur international for England as well as cricket for Lancashire. He worked for an engineering firm until one day someone found out he could write. So he wrote with all the fervour of a schoolboy, and all the balance of a highly educated man, for the *Manchester Guardian*. That's how he came to be on the plane from Belgrade, and with us in Prague some six weeks previously.

Don that trip was sharing a room on the top floor of a Prague hotel with Eric Thompson of the *Daily Mail*. The two of them immediately saw the funny side of the situation when two strong, silent characters arrived while Don was phoning his office in Manchester. The chaps told him the phone was out of order although he was using it at that very moment! So Don, ever the gentleman, allowed himself to be shepherded down the stairs to the phone box in the hall. 'Ee,' he said, 'you Communist chaps have a funny way of carrying on. I'm only sending Manchester United's team over. I've not said anything unkind about Mr Kruschev, you know.' The strong-arm chaps never smiled, they just saw Don safely to the phone booth and left him.

Later that night the phone in his room rang.

'It's out of order,' said Don.

'But this is impossible,' said a seductive voice at the other end. 'This is Natasha, you are Abdul Rachman. Remember Natasha? We have lovely time last week. You call for me now.'

Anybody less like an Arabian Abdul Rachman than the twinkling, typically British Don Davies it would be hard to find, but he replied as courteously as he could: 'I'm sorry, madam, you must have the wrong number. My name is not Abdul Rachman. This is Don Davies speaking, old international of the *Manchester Guardian*.'

Miss Natasha was now as bewildered as Don. 'Old international . . . what is this joke, sir? I wish to speak with Abdul Rachman. This is Room 505, Abdul Rachman's room, is it not?'

'This is Room 505,' said Don, 'but it is my room and Abdul Rachman is not here . . . and I'm afraid I cannot find your Arabic friend for you,' and with that he hung up.

The humour of this extraordinary conversation amused Don. 'Well, fancy coming all the way to Prague to be mistaken for an Arab,' he told us in his best and broadest Lancashire accent.

He was perhaps not surprised after he had gone to bed to be periodically wakened up by the jangling of the phone: 'Allo . . . is that Abdul Davies the cold international . . . you come quick. This is Natasha, Abdul.'

Don would hang up, chortling: 'Ee, you Press fellows are shockers.' He should have known his Press pals better than to tell them about his telephonic interlude with Natasha.

Prague? It now seemed an age ago as the memories of Don

Davies pressed on my mind. Best of all I remembered him that last night in Prague. The journalists of that city had excelled themselves in the welcome they had given us, showing us round their lovely city, the historical places of interest, the large spacious sweep of Wenceslas Square. Somehow Don didn't join in these pleasant jaunts; I think he was kept too busy making radio arrangements for his report with the BBC. So he didn't really enter into our discussions with them until after the match. One of the women journalists who was very nice and highly intelligent had trudged round the city as our guide, in heavy woollen unattractive clothes. Now she chatted vivaciously in a black velvet evening gown, pink flowers on the corsage, her head of dark hair bobbing animatedly as she talked *not* about the football match, but of her job, what Communism had done for her country, and the new part the women of Czechoslovakia were playing in rebuilding their nation. She was obviously and passionately sincere in her views. She asked us so much about England. She could not believe we had a free health service; she understood the poor in England had no food, and that they did not get proper hospital treatment, that English women were downtrodden serfs who didn't have the freedom enjoyed by the women of Prague.

Don listened attentively and then quietly broke in. 'I can quite understand you want to see changes, my dear,' he began, 'but I was in your lovely city before the First World War when it fairly bubbled with happiness, like Vienna for instance. Gay cafés, gay waltzes, full of good humour, and the churches were filled. But now it looks so sombre, recovering from the war, there is not the same joyous air about the place. Those beautiful churches look so desolate now. I don't see many people going into them. I judge a city by the faces of its children. Here I have not seen a happy child running the streets . . . they all seem to be queuing outside the shops, just like it was all over Europe in wartime. No, I'm sorry, this is not the Prague I fell in love with in 1913.'

She turned on him. 'You speak like an old man always talking of the good old days. What do you know of our struggle for equality? What do you know of the children? What things were like when the Nazis were here? You didn't see the priests and reactionaries holding back the workers from their rightful opportunities, and the equality which should be theirs. You didn't see the poor women unable to take their sick children to the hospitals because they couldn't pay for treatment.'

Don smiled tolerantly. 'Carry on, my dear. I'm sure there were inequalities which had to be altered. But what you are saying is not new. I am a worker. We are all workers. When I was at university we all talked as you do now. But we cannot be materialists all the time. Life wouldn't be worth living.' He pointed through the window at the sky like velvet, the stars glittering like minute diamonds. 'Those just didn't happen . . . they are there for a purpose like the sun, like the moon, like you and me. Carry on with your views, J——. God will understand. He always does. We don't know why children go hungry in this world, why there are sick people, why there is pain, sorrow and hardship in this world. But HE DOES.' Don's fingers were still pointing to the heavens.

Don Davies was never the man to preach to anyone about anything, he was always the type to agree to disagree, and this was one of the few times I ever saw him really opening out with his views. As I lay in that hospital bed I could picture again that kindly tolerant face all aglow, and those words: 'We don't always know why there is pain, sorrow and hardship in this world.'

What was the purpose of this air crash and all the anguish and sorrow it had caused? To the world outside it was just another accident; people were killed in the mines, on the roads, in cars and buses every day. The world carried on, as it always would.

Then one day, among the flood of letters of sympathy that poured into the Munich hospital, there was one postmarked Prague. It came from J——.

She wrote of the poignancy of the accident which she said had touched them all. They had come to look upon the Manchester United party as true friends. There had been such a comradeship with the journalists who were fellow workers and they were so wonderful and gay. She hoped that I would soon get well. How deeply sorry she was that the others who had been so vital and alive in Prague had gone. She was sorry for their families and she hoped that they had all – especially that clever and kindly little man from the *Manchester Guardian* – found everlasting peace.

Maybe Don's message that night in Prague had not been in vain.

11   Matt Busby

For a month after the crash, the news about Matt Busby was not good. He was protected from the terrible losses by an iron curtain of silence. He didn't know who had been killed; who had been injured. He lived in a half-world with his wife Jean, daughter Sheena, son Sandy and the hospital staff tensed and nervous, lest one unguarded slip of the tongue might plunge him back into the valley of despair.

Only those who visited the sick-room of the Manchester United manager knew what that meant to his family. They lived in dread; in a state of forced high spirits; while Busby husbanded his strength, calling on the reserves of that athlete's body to pull him round. He did not grumble or complain or protest or struggle or fume that ill fortune had laid him low. Busby rarely, almost never, allowed his feelings to break through that calm temperament, no matter how feverish the moments of the big sporting occasion. Nor did he now, in this his darkest hour.

The news of Matt's fight for survival was relayed to Jack Blanchflower and myself by our wives, or by Doktor Hans Gross, one of Professor Maurer's assistants who spoke English very well, and who spent many hours with Busby.

Bulletins by word of mouth were not enough. One Friday morning Sister Gilda and her squad of nurses were changing the patients' beds, and I was wheeled into the corridor. Three of them lifted me tenderly; one held my leg and the cradle in which it was slung; another gripped my arm to keep it from danger; while Sister Gilda supported me as well. It is not funny to be hawked from one bed to another like a bag of bones – but they did it in high good humour which soon dispersed the more humiliating aspect of being carried around helpless as a babe.

'Could you wheel me in to see Mr Busby, please?' I asked. Sister Gilda, that tiny efficient figure, did not understand

English, but the word Busby made her realise that it would mean something to me if I could go in to see the Boss of Old Trafford.

She wheeled me herself down the corridor and into Matt Busby's room. It was a shattering sight. He lay silent, stretched full length as though asleep, the plaster on his right leg bulging the blankets. The bushy, once sandy hair was now grey and tinged with streaks of white. The eyes opened in recognition; the pale waxy face, which belonged to a man of seventy, brightened; a thin, pitifully emaciated hand advanced haltingly over the white cover on the bed, found mine and gripped it weakly. The voice came halting and slow: 'Hallo, my old pal. How are you, Frank lad? Looks as if you're not fit for the first team yet.' Busby was physically in bad shape; there was obviously nothing wrong with his spirit. I knew then that, come what may, Busby would get well and would come back to football.

As I saw him subside weakly and gratefully back onto the pillows, I wondered whether he was thinking what I was thinking. Of the queer quirks of fate which led him from a humble miner's home in the Lanarkshire village of Orbiston to become a monarch of British Football. Of the years of painstaking effort, the careful planning, the way he had built this famous football team and breathed into them a spirit scarcely ever equalled and certainly never surpassed in the annals of British Sport. Young schoolboys with the spark of football genius in them brought to Old Trafford, carefully coached and nurtured; treated as individuals, but all loyal to the club spirit. How they rose from little more than boys into youth stars, and then were carefully groomed for the big time; until they burst like young demons on to the British Soccer scene – Roger Byrne, Duncan Edwards, Jack Blanchflower, Mark Jones, Bill Whelan, Eddie Colman, Bobby Charlton, Dennis Viollet, Tommy Taylor – household names wherever British Football is discussed. They became England's football champions with almost contemptuous ease. In 1956, and again in 1957 when they sought to bring off the fabulous treble of League Champions, FA Cup winners and European champions. Only by a hair's breadth did they fail to take the English Cup as well as the League in 1957.

They stormed across Europe, probably the greatest galaxy of

football talent ever assembled by one English club; treated as film stars wherever they went – Brussels, Bilbao, Dortmund, Berlin, Hanover, Copenhagen, Madrid, Prague. The laughing cavaliers; great ambassadors for Britain; and they had not reached their peak when the roads that led them all over Europe took them to Munich. And here, grievously stricken, lay the man who schemed and dreamed and planned that they would become great; their guide, confidant, almost like a Father Confessor to them all. And yet, how did the Busby saga begin?

They were a God-fearing family, the Busbys; and when Matt was six years of age, the eldest of four, a German sniper's bullet killed his father on the Somme.

Now the wheel had come full circle. The Germans were repaying their debt to the Busby family by fighting like furies night and day to save Matt.

Who would think, to see that poor shattered figure, that thirty years before he was a husky Scot heading south for Manchester and England and football fame. He was shy – painfully shy; his plans to become a school-teacher or to emigrate to the United States temporarily shelved, for deep down the boy had an ambition to follow in the steps of one of his schoolboy idols. A chap who lived nearby. A chap called Alex James, who even today is spoken of reverently as one of the greatest – perhaps the greatest – inside-forwards ever to play in English football.

James found it easy. Busby didn't. Everything went wrong from the day he arrived at Maine Road to join Manchester City. He wanted to be an inside-forward like his idol Alex James. He just wasn't fast enough; he hadn't that sudden devastating burst for goal. He was clever but almost too meticulous. Despair took Busby in its grip. He could see himself trekking dismally home, another young Scot who had failed in England.

Fate stepped in. Manchester City in an emergency tried him in the half-back line. There he was facing the ball as it came towards him, instead of having to turn with it, or receive passes on the half turn, or make those bewildering corkscrew bursts which are the hall-marks of the great inside-forward. At wing-half his uncanny skill with the ball saved him; he could place his passes shrewdly, methodically, as though they had all been worked out beforehand by a slide rule. At wing-half he became one of the great ones. In 1933 he was at Wembley with

Manchester City's Cup Final team. They lost to Everton 3–0; but Busby still went on playing his methodical, cultured football. A year later Manchester City were at Wembley again. Now Busby, the once so shy and nervous young Scot, had the confidence very early in the game to turn the ball back to a nineteen-year-old jittery lad in goal – just to give the kid the feel of the ball to overcome his nerves. That kid was Frank Swift. 'I never forgot that wonderful gesture by Matt,' said Frank.

That's the way Busby's mind worked. He knew just how young Swift was feeling in goal; he knew the boy wanted to get a comforting hold on the ball before he had a really serious shot to save – which he might so easily fumble. It was that same deep insight into human nature, the air of quiet confidence he bred around him, which has made him one of the great football managers of all time. And yet, as with his soccer career, Busby's managerial career began quietly enough. In 1946, with a string of wartime appearances for his country behind him, his playing career over, Busby was looking forward to continuing in the game he had enjoyed so much. He was all set to become coach to his only other League club, Liverpool. It was the sort of job where people thought that the pipe-smoking, thoughtful Scot would excel in passing on his skills to the young ones coming into the game.

Fate stepped in again. Manchester United, their ground wrecked in a wartime bombing raid, were trying to rebuild the club and they needed a young manager. The man they rather fancied was Matt Busby, even though his playing associations were with the rival club Manchester City.

Liverpool, who might so easily have said 'No', realised that this was Busby's chance to make the grade as a manager. They sportingly agreed to release him. Some folk thought Busby wouldn't have the personality to make the grade handling public relations, organising and superintending the large-scale ramifications of a modern football club. For, make no mistake, a successful football club manager needs to be as publicity-conscious as a fight promoter, or a prima donna. Astonishingly Busby, who had always seemed too quiet to attract a crowd, who preferred the quiet matter-of-fact chat to the thunderous Barnum-and-Bailey-whipped enthusiasm of the professional publicity seekers, became one of the greatest publicists of all time. Simple, really. He let the SUCCESS of his team speak for him. He argued that, in any walk of life, you must always back the class performer – no matter whether it's ballet, the stage, boxing, cycling, or soccer. Give the public first-class entertainment and they will rally round.

Busby's first Manchester United team was virtually assembled when he arrived at Old Trafford. Johnny Carey, Allenby Chilton, Stan Pearson, Johnny Morris, Jack Rowley. They were there. It needed only a few shrewd transfer buys to bring chaps like Scottish international Jimmy Delaney into the fold – and that Manchester United side became the most talked-about team in the country. Some said he was lucky; that a great playing combination had so to speak fallen into his lap. Busby said nothing. His plans were deep and well laid.

That first team, with Johnny Carey as captain, three times in succession finished runners-up in the League. In 1948 they beat Blackpool 4–2 in a Cup Final, still remembered nostalgically as the greatest-ever Football Final Wembley has ever staged. In 1952, at long last, the League Championship, which had eluded them for so long, was theirs. Students of the arts of football, who had watched and thrilled to their cultured play – the ease with which they rolled the ball from man to man as though it were being manipulated on a pin-table; the individual brilliance of players like Pearson, Aston, Cockburn and Rowley; above all the superb displays and generalship of Johnny Carey, one of the greatest club captains ever – were staggered it had taken Manchester United so long to win that title.

No sooner was the League pennant theirs than that great side started to slide. They were all getting old together. Not even a Busby could change that.

The know-alls in Sport were quite sure that this was the end of the Busby saga. He would now have to build a great team on his own – or GO BUST. They laughed when Busby solemnly announced at a club meeting that he had in fact young footballers already on his staff who one day would be valued at more than £200,000 on the transfer market – if of course he ever wanted to sell them to another club, which he certainly had no intention of doing. The bright boys, the public-house boys, gave the big horse laugh, and said of course Matt Busby was a big-head; he would never have another side as good as the one Carey captained. They were quite wrong; Busby was no big-head, he merely thought big.

Deep in that thoughtful mind he nursed the dream of creating a professional football team with a public school spirit. How could that be done? Everyone knew soccer players had their brains in their feet; once they had passed the starry-eyed stage of the teenager bursting into soccer, all they wanted was as much out of the game as they could grab before old Father Time chopped them down and they could no longer stay the pace of big-time sport. And if it meant a chap could move from club to club, perhaps picking up a little cash in some under-counter deal, what price loyalty to one club then? That was the cynic's view of soccer and soccer players. Busby figured it differently. He knew that professional soccer players actually enjoy playing soccer as much as, maybe more than, the amateurs. If you gave them a first-class set-up why should they want to move – if they were moving to play with some bums or stiffs whose only idea with a football was to kick it out of sight? Football, Busby argued, is an art; where the ball must be treated gently, coaxed and cajoled foot to foot in delicate yet forceful manoeuvres, until that ball nestles in the back of the opposing side's net. Let the crowds cheer and jeer, shout and bawl, scream with rage, laugh at the antics of the players – argue and argue and argue all week. But Busby saw it only as a challenge to produce a super team; a team that didn't allow crowds, luck, run of the ball or referees' decisions to upset its calm, methodical style of play. A style calculated to bring results not in ten weeks, but over ten years. The aim was produce not only the greatest club side in Britain – but also in Europe. Was that just a dream? Was Busby setting his sights too high?

Fate stepped in again. Way back towards the end of the war Matt Busby was in Italy where he saw a flashing-eyed Welshman who breathed with fire as he talked about football; played football; coached boys who wanted to play football. That man was Jimmy Murphy, formerly of West Bromwich Albion and Wales, and he was giving the troops coaching lessons in football. He even held Busby spell-bound. 'My first and greatest signing for Manchester United,' said Busby afterwards.

Silently, secretly, Busby gathered his back-room team together. Murphy, the miracle man with young players; Bert

Whalley, the club coach; Joe Armstrong, as sharp as a razor, who sat at the Old Trafford switchboard when he wasn't looking for young footballers. These four, and several more of the Backroom Boys, set out to search the country for the young footballers of tomorrow. Practically every other club in the First Division had the same idea – although maybe Matt Busby and his aides, along with Stan Cullis and his team of workers at Wolverhampton, were the first to really put these plans into action. To get the player when he was young; and not buy him for some huge transfer fee when he was already established in the game.

At Old Trafford they attracted a group of fine young men, many of them schoolboy internationals; others who had represented their city or town or county. First of all they needed to be football players in their own right; not kick-and-rush lads who played football as though it were the charge of the Light Brigade. They were put first of all into hand-picked lodgings, in constant touch with their families if they came from outside Manchester; they could take up a trade or be helped to join one of the professions or crafts. They were coached and encouraged to fit into the modern fluid type of play; the continental style where attack and goals count most of all; where brains mattered more than brawn; where skill counted for all so long as your side scored more goals than your opponents. Above all, these youngsters were expected to be loyal to a club tradition; they had all the benefits that football could offer. And because it was a successful club all sorts of doors were opened to them – and the emphasis was on football, football, all the time.

'Class will always tell,' Busby and his aides preached to them. And that was how slowly and gradually a team of young players was built; helped and encouraged by the older stars like Carey and Pearson and Chilton and Rowley – a young team that startled the football world and introduced a new phrase in the football follower's dictionary: THE BUSBY BABES.

How Matt hated that slick-sounding name. Sure, his team were little more than boys but they played a man's game. They were England's champions in 1956 and 1957; FA Cup runners-up and European Cup semi-finalists in 1957; and they were still not yet at their peak, these brilliant, bewildering, bumptious Busby Babes; most loved, most hated; certainly the biggest

*e last match before the
unich Air Crash, a
uropean Cup tie against
ed Star of
elgrade, on 5th
bruary, 1958. The
ams drew 3–3.*

Above: Matt Busby is greeted
on arrival in Belgrade.

Left: Tommy Taylor signs auto-
graphs for the Yugoslav fans.

Below: Some of the team
members. Left to right: Mark
Jones, Duncan Edwards, Jackie
Blanchflower, Johnny Berry.

Above: Matt Busby is interviewed by Yugoslav journalists.

Left: Tommy Taylor, followed by Duncan Edwards and Johnny Berry, leads the team out onto the waterlogged practice ground for a training session the day before the match.

Below: Roger Byrne and Dennis Viollet run out for training.

February 5th. The Busby Babes arrive at the Red Star ground for their last match.

Roger Byrne leads his team out onto the field.

The Manchester United line-up before kick-off.

Below and opposite: Manchester United in action against Red Star. Their draw put them into the next round of the European Cup on aggregate.

Members of the press who travelled with Manchester United to Belgrade preparing to board the plane at Manchester's Ringway airport. From left: Ted Ellyard (*Daily Mail*), Peter Howard (*Daily Mail*), Bert Whalley (Manchester United coach), Henry Rose (*Daily Express*) and far right, George Follows (*Daily Herald*). *Photo: Thomson Newspapers*

With my press friends the night before we crashed. From left: Alf Clarke (*Manchester Evening Chronicle*), George Follows (*Daily Herald*), Henry Rose (*Daily Express*), myself, Eric Thompson (*Daily Mail*), Tom Jackson (*Manchester Evening News*).

February 6th, 1958. A pall of
smoke sweeps across the
crashed Elizabethan airliner
near Munich airport, shortly
after the accident.
Photo: Daily Mirror

This house at the
end of the runway
was set ablaze
when the
Elizabethan
crashed into it.
Here firemen go to
work amid the
scattered
wreckage.
Photo: Daily Mirror

The twisted
remains of the
crashed aircraft. Of
the 44 people on
board, only 21
survived.

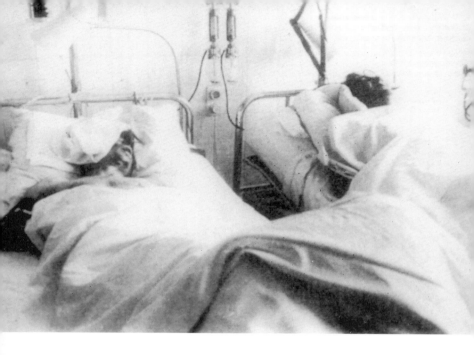

The crash victims were taken to the Rechts der Isar Hospital in Munich. Here John Berry (left) lies beside Duncan Edwards who later died from his injuries.

My right leg and left arm were badly broken.

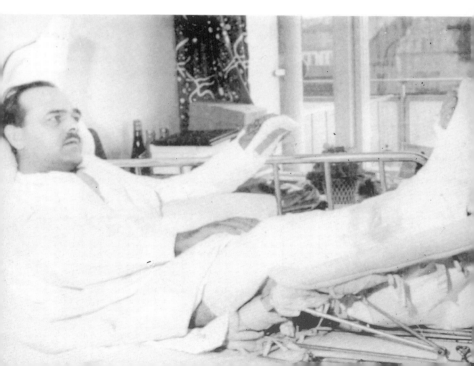

My wife Peggy makes me comfortable. With other wives and relatives of the victims, she was flown out as soon as my survival had been confirmed.
Photo: Daily Mail

Manchester United were to have played Wolverhampton Wanderers two days after the crash. The match was cancelled, but the Wolves team lined up at the ground to pay its respects to those who died.
Photo: Derek G. Johnson

Players of Tottenham Hotspur and Manchester City stand in silent tribute. The scene was repeated at soccer and rugby matches throughout Britain on the Saturday following the accident, and in Europe the next day.

A month after the accident, Manchester United Football Club entertained Professor George Maurer and his staff from the Rechts der Isar Hospital, in gratitude for their treatment of the crash victims. A recorded message from Matt Busby was relayed over the ground, where United were playing West Bromwich Albion. *Photo: Keystone Press Agency*

On the hospital verandah with Maria Spitzener, the medical orderly who took the telephone call announcing the crash.

Father Angelo P. O'Hagan, the monk who became my good friend during the long months in hospital.

THE BUSBY BABES WHO SURVIVED THE CRASH

Bobby Charlton in 1960.
Photo: Central Press Photos

Charlton in action in 1970.
Photo: Colin Elsey

Dennis Viollet at the time of the accident.
Photo: Universal Pictorial Press

Viollet in action in 1959.
Photo: Sunday Mirror

Jackie Blanchflower in 1957.
Photo: Central Press Photos

Blanchflower in action, at the time of his first international for Ireland in 1954. *Photo: PA-Reuter Photos*

Harry Gregg, United's
goalkeeper in 1959.
Photo: Fox Photos

Gregg in action six months
after the crash.
Photo: Central Press Photos

Return to Belgrade. I meet fellow survivor Nebosja Tomasevich, the Yugoslav diplomat who now edits the *Yugoslav Review* and is the author of many art books.

Outside Buckingham Palace in March, 1979, when H.M. the Queen presented me with the OBE for services to sport. *Photo: Press Association*

attraction in the game. Remember them as they played in Belgrade:

Gregg, Foulkes, Byrne, Colman, Jones, Edwards, Morgans, Viollet, Taylor, Charlton, Scanlon. And on the side-lines equally brilliant players fighting for a place like Billy Whelan, Jackie Blanchflower, David Pegg, Johnny Berry, Wilf McGuinness, Freddie Goodwin, Ray Wood, and so many more.

Do you remember them? Come, let's leave Matt Busby, the man who built that team, pale and weary, recuperating from his grievous blows. Let's tiptoe out of his sick-room and leave him alone with his memories. I would like to tell you about his lads and of their soccer journeys which led them across Europe and ended on an airfield at MUNICH.

12 The Rise of the Red Devils

It all began in the summer of 1956, the year Manchester United, with an average age of just over twenty, won the English League Championship, and were invited to enter a new competition open to the élite clubs on the continent. The European Cup. A year previously Chelsea, who had won the English Championship, had been asked to join this tourney. They turned it down, it was alleged, through pressure from high authority. There was no doubt that some prominent voices in the Football League and the Football Association saw in this competition a deadly foe to home football. That once the public saw the fantastic skills of some of these continentals, they would ask for, and expect, higher standards from the professional clubs over here.

Manchester United, when they won the title, were, like Chelsea, urged to turn down the chance of taking part in Europe's Cup. United's directors and manager Matt Busby thought they had a side young enough and good enough to take on the best of Europe, and in the process to re-establish this country as the tops of the sport they gave to the world. They felt, and how right they were, that this competition glittered with gold as well as prestige. In a few short months people were fighting and clamouring to get tickets for these glamorous cup ties under the floodlights.

Thus did England's young champions set sail on their voyage of discovery on the sometimes stormy soccer seas of Europe. They were football's adventurers, explorers, for no other English League club before them had pitted their skills against the top continental sides in a knockout competition as distinct from friendlies. These were challenge matches; sudden death for those who weren't good enough.

Manchester United's first port of call was Brussels in September 1956 to play Anderlecht, the champions of Belgium; managed by a homespun Lancastrian, Bill Gormlie, who one time kept goal for Blackburn Rovers. That first game bore no hint of the fantastic return match to follow. It was distinguished chiefly by a tremendous performance from Jackie Blanchflower, United's jack-of-all-positions, who came in as a late understudy for the injured Duncan Edwards at left-half, and promptly set Brussels afire with a glittering display which made him the man of the match and was the biggest single factor in United's narrow victory.

The game could easily have gone either way. The return at Maine Road, Manchester, went only one way – towards the Anderlecht goal – as England's super-champions ripped the ball ten times into their net.

That match was played on Manchester City's ground, because United had not yet erected their magnificent flood-lighting system. Some 43,635 spectators saw the match; and they never saw anything like this before, nor are they likely to again, in my opinion. On a pitch studded with pools of water, which made conditions more suitable for water polo than soccer, the Red Devils played punishing football which would have beaten any club side in the world. It was a night when everything they tried came off; when the ball sped from man to man as though it were moved by some magnetic influence. Ten goals in ninety minutes of football; that sort of score would have made news had a First Division club thrashed an English Fourth Division side by the same score in an FA cup tie. Yet this Anderlecht team were a great side; they had not become Belgian champions without some pretence to class and skill. Week, in the Anderlecht goal, didn't know what day it was as goals poured past him from Dennis Viollet (4), Tommy Taylor (3), Bill Whelan (2) and Johnny Berry. The only man in the forward line who didn't score was the best forward of the five, David Pegg, who was too busy making touchline runs to create goals for the others, to score himself.

The crowd were delirious at the end of ninety minutes, seeing goal after goal thud into the net in what was a savage soccer slaughter. Anderlecht, sportsmen to the last gasp, clapped and applauded their conquerors all the way to the dressing-rooms, while an unbelieving, incredulous Matt Busby, still reeling from this onslaught by his team, could only mutter: 'It was the greatest thrill in a lifetime of soccer. It was the finest exhibition of team work I have ever seen from any team – club or international. It was as near perfect football as anyone could wish to see.'

Machine soccer murdered the Anderlecht team; but the all-too-cocky Busby boys nearly shot out of the Cup in the next round when they took on the West German champions, Borussia Dortmund. Thousands poured into Maine Road on the night of October 17th, 1956, expecting another goal glut.

It looked that way for thirty-five minutes as Viollet (2) and Pegg scored. This was going to be another Anderlecht; or so the fans thought. But a chap with the kittenish-sounding name of Kwiatkowski played like a cat in the Dortmund goal. He had borrowed a green jersey from his fellow countryman Bert Trautmann, the Manchester City goalkeeper, for the occasion; and not even bounding Bert Trautmann played better than this.

The cock-a-hoop United were just a trifle too contemptuous of the opposition. Roger Byrne, instead of clearing the ball, breasted it down nonchalantly for goalkeeper Wood – and Kapitulski did the rest. Roger held his head in disgust. A few minutes later the whole defence were disgusted when another daft mistake gave the fighting Germans a second goal. Would that one goal margin be enough to keep United in the Cup when they travelled to the Ruhr for the return? No man was more determined that United would win through than the club's captain, Roger Byrne. After that first match he parried critics with: 'Yes, it was a silly mistake on my part – but don't you ever make mistakes?'

Roger Byrne was one of the most misunderstood men in football. The fans fought and fumed and howled at him, 'Cocky Byrne' – 'Bighead Byrne'; they booed him when he petulantly kicked the ball into touch to delay the taking of a free kick; but those who were close to him knew him as a great player, a wonderful captain and a first-class sportsman. In fact, Byrne was a superb gamesman who, although he was never a great tackler and his heading ability was scarcely past amateur stage, made himself into an international footballer of the highest repute by concentrated effort, careful study, and constant application. An educated man, he studied football as others might study maths; he weighed up each opponent's tricks and had them carefully tabulated and filed in his mind. I saw him in many incidents on the football fields; appealing strongly to the referees; carefully marshalling a wall of defenders to block a free kick; little tricks and dodges which drove crowds on away grounds nearly frantic with rage. But I never, in all the times I watched him, saw Roger Byrne guilty of a nasty foul on an opponent. He was proud of his calling as a professional footballer; any of his little stratagems were designed with one object in view – to help his team. He was unreservedly and wholeheartedly a 100 per cent trier, whether he played for his club or his country.

That's why Byrne smarted at the indignity he had caused his club by one lackadaisical moment in that game with Borussia. He meant to rub that blot out of the book. And he did.

Some 7,000 British Army lads flocked to Dortmund to see the game, and United almost skidded out of the Cup before the start. The pitch was rather like a skating rink, and they had no rubber studs with them. Trainer Tom Curry did a hasty cobbling job in the dressing-rooms, fitting the boots with short studs. Even their best friends would say United looked anything but champions that night. They slipped and slithered trying to control that impish ball, while the Germans pussyfooted about the pitch stroking the ball with contemptuous ease. Dennis Viollet, small and neat and very fast, might have scored in such conditions, but he was hurt. Massive Duncan Edwards moved up from the half-back line to take his place, with Wilf McGuinness at left-half detailed to watch the Dortmund scheming genius, Mr Preissler. As the old-gold shirts of Dortmund fluttered round United's goal like moths round a flame, Roger Byrne never put a foot wrong. He, Ray Wood in goal, Billy Foulkes, McGuinness and the stout-hearted Mark Jones, refused to give in when all seemed lost. The night was so cold that Wood had on his track-suit trousers tucked in his stockings, which gave him the appearance of a navvy. He worked like one. At the end neither side had scored, and no wonder. Ice-cool Johnny Carey never played better than did Roger Byrne that night. He flicked the ball forward to try and get the attack rolling; and when the heat was on and United needed a breather, he had no compunction but booted the ball high and heartily into the crowd. I don't think he missed a tackle or hit a wrong ball in all the ninety minutes and all the time he was shouting and waving his arms – like a scene from one of those old Victorian prints where the general is enthusiastically waving his troops into action – inspiring, cajoling and encouraging his team-mates to stand fast.

At the social banquet after the game one of the players, altogether too excited, lost his temper and was a little too insulting to a Pressman. Byrne proved his quality as a captain by seeking out the journalist. 'I hope you'll accept my apology for So-and-so on behalf of the whole team. He is a little excited after the game, and he doesn't really mean what he said. Tomorrow he'll be upset when he recalls this little outburst – so I'm saying sorry for him tonight, to save any misunderstandings.' That was Byrne, a far-seeing diplomatic captain the crowds didn't know.

I chatted with Roger Byrne as we flew back from Dortmund with United safely into the quarter-finals of the European Cup. 'Well, Rog, you've settled that score with Dortmund. You certainly made amends for that gift goal you gave them at Maine Road,' I said.

Byrne looked embarrassed. 'Yes, they certainly made us go. But wasn't Mark Jones great? I think if Dortmund had had a tank at centre-forward he'd have stopped that – and nothing could have got past Ray Wood.'

Byrne was right; but the greatest of all that night in the Ruhr was Byrne, the captain courageous.

England's roving soccer ambassadors had just about six weeks to keep in trim for the next big game in the Cup, in the Basque country of the Iberian peninsula. As long as I live I shall never forget the matches Manchester United played against Bilbao. In the 180 minutes of these games, twenty-two superbly fit men ploughed through fearful slush and mud; scored eleven goals; and the football was played at a heart-tugging speed as the goal-drunk crowds howled for goals and still more goals.

We flew from Ringway on a frosty morning, January 15th, 1957, in a Dakota that plugged along sedately like a hansom cab. The plane commander, Captain Riley, was undecided at first whether to refuel in the Channel Islands or to push ahead for Bordeaux. He decided to make France the first stop, so we flew down the western seaboard of France, with the Atlantic heaving and rolling far below us, the waves white-topped, fearsome and angry. The heating system in the aeroplane broke down, and the club chairman, seventy-five-old Mr Harold Hardman, bravely tried to smile and keep cheerful, although it was plain to see the cold and the bumpy flight were not altogether pleasurable to him. Another youthful energetic figure looked pretty morose too. That was Duncan Edwards, a titan on the football field, but not the best of air travellers. When the plane was refuelled at Bordeaux the heating system was rectified, and as we got aboard the sudden surge of heat had an immediate effect on Edwards. As we flew out over the angry-looking bay on the last hop to Bilbao, big Duncan sat alone, silent and apprehensive.

'What's the matter, Duncan?' I asked.

'Too hot for me. I shall be air-sick,' came the reply of a man who didn't want to talk.

'Get the heater turned off, man, if you feel that bad.'

'No,' he replied. 'The chairman has been feeling the cold. Leave me alone. I'll be all right.'

As the Dakota nosed onward towards the Spanish coast, the big lad was quite groggy. We flew on until it seemed we were within wing-tip-touching distance of the huge cliffs which prodded out to sea. We flew a few miles like that, until an opening in the rocky coast indicated Bilbao was coming up on the port side. We came in anxiously, over the huddle of ships in the harbour, the cranes and works at the docks, with the hills all round dusted in snow. Once, twice, three times the captain circled the plane as we looked down anxiously to spot the runway. Eventually we could see a single strip almost like a river, until Captain Riley pointed the nose down and the aeroplane swept down to land. Then we saw one end of the runway was covered with water but dry at the other end. Weather conditions were bad. The airfield had been closed; but the Consul staff, hearing the plane overhead, realised it was the Manchester United team, so the assistant consul drove down at high speed in his car to make sure the field was opened and the airport staff ready to receive the plane. We plopped down nicely and easily in a spume of spray, and taxied up to the airfield buildings.

Eddie Colman was one of the first out of the plane and he nearly fell flat on his face. '*Carramba!*' he shouted in high good humour. 'Salford was never like this.'

The rest of the boys surveyed the white-topped hills and the dusting of snow. 'Sunny Spain? Blimey, let's get back to sunny Manchester.'

Duncan Edwards still looked like a man who had had gastric 'flu. Sensing a story, I quizzed him: 'Do you think you'll be fit to play on Wednesday, Duncan?'

He was thunderstruck and looked at me as though I was mad. 'Miss the match? What do you take me for – a sissy?' And with that he staggered away, still pretty wobbly at the knees. He played all right, in a game which turned out to be more like a commando toughening-up exercise than a football match. In my report for the *News Chronicle* at the time I wrote of Edwards thus: '. . . what a joy for English hearts to see Duncan Edwards the blockbuster biting hard in the tackle and shoving the ball through with far-flung accurate passes.'

Edwards had recovered his land legs all right.

Bilbao had lost only one match on their own ground in three years; and the way they played it was not hard to realise why. The snow came down in little fluffy balls, like cotton wool. On the far side of the pitch from the Press box there stretched a long wide terrace, without semblance of cover. On that desolate piece of ground there gathered thousands of brave Spanish football fans armed with black umbrellas, looking for all the world like an army of Civil Servants on parade. Up went the umbrellas in a vast black forest, which heaved and swayed with the movement of the game, the black gradually turning to white as the snow covered them.

The match began with high drama. From the kick-off a quick passing move ended with Dennis Viollet speeding like an arrow through the middle. His shot was going like a rocket into the net when, incredibly, it stuck in the mud on the goal-line. Frantically the Spaniards booted it upfield, where Mark Jones, solid, imperturbable, dependable as ever, moved forward to take it and start another United attack. He slipped, and in a threshing jumble of arms and legs the ball bounced from him to Artiche, the Bilbao centre-forward, who moved on as a man in a dream, disbelieving such a gift. That was one up for Spain. Poor Mark Jones, who always played for the team and never for Mark Jones, nearly wept. He was inconsolable afterwards, blaming himself quite wrongly for giving a goal away in so vital a match. It was purely and simply a slip. As the play bubbled and frothed there was a scene of pure farce in the Press box. Tom Jackson of *Manchester Evening News* had spent long hours checking and rechecking that the phone arrangements were in order. He had been to the British Consul and to the telephone technicians to make quite sure that there was no likelihood of a hitch and that Manchester evening papers would get their reports of the game which had so captured public imagination.

Tom sat sturdily one end of the box; Alf Clarke, his friend and rival evening newspaperman, at the other. Both picked up their phones and started to dictate the scene and that early shock goal. They were jabbering away trying to convey the white-hot moments of this tremendous struggle, until Tom eventually got fed up with a voice chattering away on the same line. After shouting for this intruder on his phone to shut up, he quietly got up from his seat and walked to the far end of the box and tapped Alf Clarke on the shoulder.

'I say, Alf.'

'Go away, Tom. Can't you see I'm on the phone to the sports desk sending this running report? Now go away, you ought to know better.'

Journalists, who have to fight and plan like mad to make sure they can get their copy back to their offices in time to catch editions, will appreciate Alf Clarke's feeling as Tom Jackson tapped him again on the shoulder and said with a sad shake of his head: 'You're not speaking to the *Evening Chronicle* at all, Alf. You are sending your report to me at the other end of the box – and the voice you could hear shouting back at you was mine.'

Tom laughed uproariously as Alf gazed unbelievingly. Then they both made a dive for the interpreter to get the telephone situation disentangled. Fortunately, in a matter of minutes they were able to contact their offices. They were lucky. It could quite easily have gone the other way, for fixing up telephones is just one of the major snags the sports writer abroad faces when he tries to do a snap story from the football ground itself.

While this comic – yet highly critical – interlude was going on in the Press box, stark disaster faced England's champions on the football field. At half-time they were 3–0 down, and Matt Busby and his chief assistant Jimmy Murphy stalked serious-faced into the dressing-room to try and evolve some tactical plan to rectify the situation. Amazingly enough, within eight minutes of the re-start they were back in the game with the score now 3–2. Tommy Taylor, the lad from Barnsley, lithe of limb, tall and dark-haired, moved through the slush and mud with the grace of a gazelle to lead this revival. His thrilling tussles with Garay, one of the best centre-halves in Europe, were pure joy to see. Taylor chased and chivvied to get the ball, inspiring the other forwards by his never-give-up attitude; then, alarmingly, United slumped again through slack defence and Bilbao were coasting home at 5–2. United had given their all to get those two goals; now, in the treacly mud, they were finished. Everyone said so. They were surely out of the European Cup, for how could they possibly hope to play on their own ground three goals down, and try to score the four goals necessary if they were to win the tie on aggregate? No, Busby's invincibles were smashed, battered, beaten. Nothing could save them now. But hold on, five minutes to go, and here is Billy Whelan, the quiet boy from Dublin, on the ball in his own half. When Whelan had the ball under control like that he was always liable to make it do anything but talk. That weird shuffle; the sudden quickening of speed; the rolling shoulders hunched over the ball, protecting it lovingly; the pull back with the ball; the sudden feints and stops; the crazy corkscrew turns that bore no resemblance to sleek well-balanced athletic movement; but when Whelan did it on a football field it could be quite devastating.

He took the ball now, lazily, and started to dribble, coaxing it along through the waves of mud, beating first one man, then another, gradually gathering pace all the time. A shrug of the shoulders; a jink and turn and a change of direction until he had wriggled his way diagonally across-field from right to left, then started to come back again into the middle, leaving a trail of bewildered Bilbaoans in his wake. For more than forty yards the wandering Whelan took the ball until one wondered how he had the strength after such a hard slogging match; or whether in fact he would ever muster the strength to draw back his foot and try to shoot. Whelan ploughed on until Carmelo came out of his goal, and from a spot just inside the penalty area Whelan hit the ball hard and true into the top left-hand corner of the net. A goal to remember in any conditions. In this murderous mud, a miracle goal that kept United's European Cup hopes alive. But only just.

Bilbao looked bleak on the Thursday after the match as we took the coach to the flying strip. We found the plane coated with snow and ice with a ground engineer flown out specially from England working feverishly to get it serviceable. The players volunteered to help and marched out like a fatigue party, with brooms and shovels on their shoulders in 'OPERATION SNOW SHIFT'. The crew, including Radio Officer Potter, were on the job too; and with mist and low cloud about Captain Riley couldn't say when we could fly back to Manchester. Just as the players were settling down for lunch after clearing the snow, there was a mad scramble. The clouds had lifted momentarily, and flying conditions were as near perfect as they were ever likely to be that day. If we didn't move fast there was always the chance the cloud formations would close in again, and we would be stranded in northern Spain. That would never do. United had a League match on the Saturday against Sheffield Wednesday at Hillsborough. At all costs they must get back for that.

The players, officials and Press flung themselves aboard the aircraft, and we zoomed down the runway out towards the sea. We flew up the coast of France into sunnier weather, and so to the Channel Islands for refuelling. As we came in to Jersey over the sea we appeared to be dropping short of the runway. With a sudden late burst of power from the engines the plane lifted at the last moment over the cliffs and the hedges and dropped down safely and smoothly on to the runway.

'Close thing that,' muttered Johnny Berry. He was to remind me of that momentary alarm just over a year later in Munich.

The return match with Bilbao at Maine Road, Manchester, was not a masterly display of football skill. It couldn't be. Bilbao came with one idea in mind. They were two goals to the good; they brought every one back on defence. Their motto: 'They shall not pass.' The result was a game which in my experience was the most thrilling I've ever reported. Which club could hope to give another first-class side two goals start and then beat them? It was as though Wolves had undertaken not only to beat Arsenal on their own ground, but to guarantee to do it by three clear goals.

That was the target Busby's team faced as Manchester

seethed and pulsed at the prospect. The roar of Manchester's thousands came like a clap of thunder as the Red Devils ran out with ninety minutes to score three goals. They began like a racing-car geared up for a top-speed getaway; but they were too fast, too eager for tidy football. The crowd lost their pre-match feverish enthusiasm, and grunted and groaned as chance after chance was missed. In his touchline seat Matt Busby lost his usual composure. He writhed and wriggled and squirmed and smoked cigarette after cigarette to try and soothe his tattered nerves. Frantically, as half-time neared, he waved Duncan Edwards to go upfield to lend his power and thunderbolt shot to the barrage. Four minutes before the break Edwards struck, a screaming drive which was speeding towards the net till Garay stuck out a despairing foot. The ball flew to Dennis Viollet – and United now needed only two goals to win the tie.

The interval dragged on interminably as the crowd fretted – only forty-five minutes to go. Could United grab those two goals? The game restarted at its now familiar pace. Within minutes the crowd thundered its applause. Viollet had scored. No, he hadn't. The German referee Albert Deutsch had whistled for offside. A minute later Whelan had the ball in the net. GOAL! No, Mr Deutsch, right up with play, gave another offside decision against United. The crowd hollered that United were being robbed, that fate was unkind – but Mr Deutsch never faltered. He knew he was right. The crowd ranted and raved and chanted and cheered as these never-give-up Busby Boys crammed on even more pressure. Now it was Tommy Taylor's great moment. The big centre-forward, often criticised as a flop as England's leader, took the game by the scruff of the neck and shook it till victory was won.

In the seventieth minute he swerved like a ballet dancer round the masterly Garay, and shot hard and fiercely with his left foot. Carmelo's clutching fingers failed to touch the ball but with the Spanish keeper grovelling on the ground beaten, the ball thudded against the post and was cleared. Saved by a post! Would United's luck never change? A minute later the tear-away Taylor sailed past Garay again. This time his shot beat Carmelo and there was no woodwork to stop it going into the net. The score was now 2–0, and United were whipped into a frenzy trying to get that extra goal which would give them victory complete and absolute. If it stayed 2–0 they would have to replay in Paris.

Five minutes to go, and still brave Bilbao kept them out, until Taylor, with his dark mane streaming in the wind, moved out to the right touchline with Garay at his shoulder like a policeman. Taylor, with the ball at his feet, suddenly found that extra yard of pace which took him past Garay and he sped swiftly for the corner flag. What to do now? Take a chance and come inside for an angled shot at goal? No, hold it, Tommy. Little Johnny Berry, anticipating the move, had raced from the right wing to Taylor's position at centre-forward, and he stood there waving and shouting for the ball. Gently, ever so gently, Tommy Taylor rolled it back carefully and accurately. Johnny Berry's right foot did the rest. In seconds he was engulfed by his delirious colleagues; the roars of the crowd rolled over Manchester, wave after wave of them; they sang and they cheered and they tore on to the field to hail a victory for British Football, for British guts.

Along the touchline Matt Busby, soccer's Mr Poker Face, did a jig of joy with *his* right-hand man Jimmy Murphy, who wept tears of joy. 'Damn' silly, isn't it?' said Murphy, who hides a heart of gold under a gruff exterior. 'Damn' silly after all these years in the game. But this is my greatest game in football.'

The heroes of the hour hadn't a word to say. They were too tired to do anything but sit in the steaming baths and soak and soak and soak and think of that European Cup semi-final date in Madrid.

That gay night in Manchester for the Bilbao game was one of the greatest ever for the Busby Boys. The date was February 6th, 1957, twelve months precisely from the Munich Air Crash.

13   United Miss that Treble

Real Madrid, at their best, could have taken on any team in the world. Had it been possible for them to have entered the World Cup, they would probably have won it.

This may seem an extravagant claim to modern football fans, who have been brought up to admire the discipline and the consistency of teams such as Liverpool, Bayern Munich, and others.

It is only when you study their record that the true picture of their staggering skill emerges. They won the European Cup six times, including that epic victory over Eintracht Frankfurt at Hampden Park, which many experts rate the best game ever seen in the British Isles.

Jimmy Murphy, I think gave the best assessment of Real Madrid when I was writing the book *Matt, United and Me* with him. When we came to Real Madrid Jimmy said: 'Everyone in Britain is forever quoting the great Hungarian side. They were great, though they never won the World Cup, but Real Madrid were not only great, they were consistent with it . . .'

When United were drawn to play Real Madrid in the European Cup semi-finals in 1957, Busby wanted to have a close look at them beforehand. I flew with him to Nice in the Spring of 1957, and what an eye opener that was! Matt studied the play of Alfredo di Stefano, a centre-forward who appeared to cover every blade of grass on the field, before commenting, 'Until today I thought Alex James and Peter Doherty were the two best inside forwards I had ever seen. But now I have seen Alfredo the Great . . . he's in a class of his own.'

Apart from di Stefano, Real had other great stars, such as Gento, a left winger with the pace of an Olympic sprinter; Mateos who goaded opponents like a matador; and Kopa the Frenchman who had all the skills.

Busby prepared his players for the great game, and in April

we flew to Madrid in an Elizabethan for the first match, piloted, ironically, by Captain Ken Rayment.

Madrid was afire for the game. The sun beat down mercilessly as the Spaniards besieged the plane at the airfield, dark-haired, flashing-eyed señoritas among them, eager to see this wonder team from England. The Busby Boys wore their usual club blazers and typically English flannels with flashy grey trilbies, which made them conspicuous on the streets. They couldn't move without a swarm of admirers or autograph-hunters. Wisely they spent many hours resting for the ordeal ahead, away from the sun and the crowds.

At the hotel, there was an incessant call for Mr Taylor. I answered the phone and was greeted by a husky, charming feminine voice which said: 'Ah, Mr Taylor, you are the Manchester United centre-forward Tommy Taylor. This is one of the flamenco dancers from Mr Antonio's troupe. We have entertained your club with our dancing, is it possible you have a ticket for tomorrow's match?'

I broke in hastily: 'Madam, I am not the United centre-forward, heaven forbid.' And I hastily passed the call over to Tommy Taylor who, like all the players, was being pestered every minute of the day for tickets.

A football match at the Bernabeu Stadium in Madrid is a glittering occasion. This is a millionaire setting; tier upon tier of terraces, lifted skywards like a huge sugar cake. Here the poor boys – and some rich ones too – come to play all sports. They keep a record of every individual's performance at running, jumping, weight-lifting, gymnastics, basket ball. Under the stands they have a dentist's room, a surgery, even a mortuary and a chapel, all laid out artistically and with grace. There are no covered grandstands because it does not rain often in Madrid.

A small dapper Spanish gentleman, who announced that he was a supporter of the club, showed Frank Swift and myself round the place. Not until later did I find out that he was the El Conde de Gerena. Real Madrid is that sort of club; with those sort of supporters.

On the day of the match a sweating, feverish throng poured in their thousands to the stadium, jamming the streets, and I was told that as there are no turnstiles, a man with a ticket often pushed through and one or two friends piled in after him on the same ticket. Be that as it may, over 120,000 was the official attendance returned, and no other British League club has ever played before a crowd like that before.

From the Press box the ground looked like a concrete ant-hill; and down below us the peasants squirted their wine into their mouths, passing the containers from man to man, and even into the Press box itself. Geoffrey Green of *The Times* and Archie Ledbrooke of the *Mirror* both drank the wine Spanish fashion, with a quick squeeze of the container, which sent a stream of liquid into the mouth. The more clumsy merely drenched their shirts instead of hitting the target of their mouths.

As soon as the game started it was apparent what Busby's trump card was. The man he set to mark the maestro di Stefano was not the powerful Duncan Edwards, as most people had imagined it would be, but the little man, Eddie Colman. A peseta millionaire, all airs and graces, policed by a humble, but nevertheless highly mobile and brilliant, footballer from Salford, which is not exactly the most wealthy or salubrious of places.

The pattern of the game was easy to see. Real Madrid played gay, artistic, colourful football, rolling the ball accurately from one white shirt to another. United played it English style. No nonsense, hard tackling, not so fast or so elegant as Madrid, but eminently practical.

It was football played in fiesta mood, with Madrid taking a smooth two-goal lead which brought out the John Bull in the Manchester men. At one stage Madrid lost their poise, and Jack Blanchflower was abominably chased and fouled, which in England would have sent the culprit to the dressing-room.

Gento on the left wing struck with rapier speed time and time again. Byrne at left-back was an iceberg in the heat; Duncan Edwards like the Rock of Gibraltar; little Colman chased di Stefano as though he were a long-lost brother; while Jackie Blanchflower padlocked the middle as though he were a gaoler. Yet always the white shirts flitted about the field like ghosts, an untouchable, unforgettable soccer machine that ran on jewelled movements. Tommy Taylor lashed himself into a fury – as he generally did in these games – moving with the grace of one of the Madrid men. Higher praise than that I cannot give. At one point England's champions pulled the score dramatically back to 2–1 through a Tommy Taylor goal. With luck it might have ended that way, until a three-prong move between Gento, Mateos and Riall ended with the ball ricocheting from them to Billy Foulkes and back to Mateos, who drove it in for a 3–1 score. A lucky bounce? Yes, but Real Madrid looked what they were, the greatest club side in Europe. A side good enough to take on any international side in the World Cup.

United flew back to Britain for a League match at Luton, and in the following weeks strode majestically on, to win the League and reach the Cup Final. In between came the return with Madrid.

This was an anticlimax after the all-action Bilbao match which had preceded it. But it served one significant purpose: it illumined the vast gap between top-class continental soccer and the best in Britain. Our football supporters are satiated with the big boys who batter and crash their way through a marathon Cup and League programme. These brawny boys at times look like carthorses in the Derby when pitted against the fleet-footed agile artists on the continent. Maybe we have been kidded by the blood-and-thunder shoulder charges; the huge men who plough through the mud heaps in mid-winter; the big kickers and the crowds who bay for results at all costs and forget the finer points of football. Sometimes our soccer looks like the almighty slash of a sabre against the quick-moving points of the rapier. And on the green fields, firm grounds, and referees who frown on charging the goalkeeper, our footballers, when they play against the slick movers from abroad, look like a matador who has strayed inadvertently into a ballet class. It is really a question of what sort of football you like to see – artistry, or sheer power.

Madrid, when they came to Manchester, didn't fall into the same trap as Bilbao. For twenty minutes they were quite content to let the Red Devils run into a brick wall; they employed every dodge within the law to let England's champions sap their strength, their energy and their will to win. Free kick followed free kick until the experienced Spanish team struck with the speed of lightning. Gento was their man. One goal came from Kopa, another from di Stefano. The 60,000 crowd at Old Trafford were silenced by these mastermen from Madrid. It was all so simple, so easy – so artistic.

People from all walks of life were at the ground eager to see Manchester United win for England; Cyril Washbrook, the Lancashire and England cricketer, was one; Tom Finney, of Preston North End and England, was another. Both declared that for the night they were Manchester United supporters.

Sheer fighting spirit brought Manchester United back into the game, first with a goal by Viollet, then another from Taylor. The crowd hooted and roared, hoping that United could bring off the impossible by giving Real Madrid, the aristocrats of European football, a two-goal start, and then win on aggregate. Not even Busby's brilliant young men could do that. As the game died Mateos collapsed after a tackle, and was hustled off the field by Duncan Edwards. The Madrid team were glad to kick high and anywhere – but like true champions they withstood the assault.

United had failed in their bid for the Soccer Treble. They were out of the European Cup. But could they still win the FA Cup and add that to the League title already won to make it a *fantastic football double*? No club had won Cup and League since Aston Villa did it in 1899 – and before that the Old Preston Invincibles in 1888. With fewer matches it was easier then – could the New Invincibles of England achieve that elusive double – the first club to do so in this century?

The worst moment in United's bid for the FA Cup occurred on the Hartlepool ground, when they strolled casually to a three-goal lead on that tiny pitch, and then were suddenly struggling desperately at 3–3. One man saved the day. His name? Bill Whelan. He ploughed through the heavy mud and scored the vital fourth goal which saved the champions at a time when they were reeling to defeat.

I was at that match and saw Whelan, the hero of the hour, sit disconsolately in the coach afterwards, travel sick – a combination of reaction after a hard-fought match, and the long journey by road. He was never the best of road travellers. The skipper, Roger Byrne, sat with him the whole way, joking and talking to him. Once more, United's young and thoughtful captain had come to the aid of a team-mate.

Slowly, almost inevitably, the young champions coasted towards Wembley. They had a grave scare when Tommy Taylor, who took so much punishment uncomplainingly at centre-forward, developed a crack in the shinbone. Bravely he tried to carry on, until eventually even this happy warrior of the football fields had to give way.

When semi-final day dawned at Hillsborough, Sheffield, against the redoubtable Birmingham City, Matt Busby tried the then revolutionary tactic of playing his inside-left, the light-weight Dennis Viollet, at centre-forward, with a young thunderbolt shooting star, by name Bobby Charlton, at inside-left.

Viollet had himself been nursing a recurring groin injury all season, and it was hard to see him operating successfully at centre-forward. Matt Busby figured that Viollet, one of the unsung highly competent players of the age, was such a perfect positional player that he would cause the hard-tackling Birmingham side, who had been losing finalists at Wembley the previous year, no end of worry. It worked out that way.

Charlton, with an acrobatic shot on the half-turn which came from a man who looked agile enough to be part of a high-wire trapeze act, and another by Berry, won the game in the opening twenty minutes. After that United closed the shutters. They were through to Wembley and they hoped Tommy Taylor would be fit by then. He was. Unfortunately Viollet wasn't.

Close observers of the soccer scene will always wonder how it came about that Manchester United, the hottest favourites for years, should have failed to add the FA Cup to the League title they had already won. They should have done. They didn't because of an unlucky accident which, although sad, is what makes football so attractive a game.

When he travelled down to London with me, Matt Busby confessed: 'Nothing is sure in football, but it is hard to see how we can lose against Aston Villa. They are a hard side, but Wembley favours the ball players and not the tough tacklers. I think we have more ball players and we should win this match through our wingers.'

Busby didn't count on one of those cruel accidents, which prevented the Cup from coming to Old Trafford. For one thing he couldn't play the experienced Dennis Viollet. In the opening exchanges the inexperienced Bobby Charlton might have scored – then after six minutes came an incident which is for evermore engraved on FA Cup history.

Villa made a sudden swoop down the right wing, and the ball was flung high and hard towards the left, where the powerful Peter McParland was waiting some dozen yards from goal. At that range it would have needed an extraordinary header to beat a goalkeeper, and though the ball fairly rocketed off the Irishman's head, Ray Wood caught it quite easily on his goal-line, and advanced two steps. McParland, a strong and robust player, raced in to challenge with a shoulder charge, working presumably on the assumption that no goalkeeper likes to be rattled early in such a nerve-jangling ordeal as a Cup Final. McParland missed with his first rush, but turning swiftly came alongside Wood, and essayed a shoulder charge, McParland's left shoulder against Wood's right. There was a fearful crack as Wood, still holding the ball, appeared to turn into the Villa man, apparently unaware he was there, for there seemed no reason why the goalkeeper couldn't have kicked the ball up-field.

Instead, both players crashed to the turf, Wood rolling over and over in agony as Matt Busby joined his trainer Tom Curry, both running across the field to see what fearful accident had happened. Wood's jaw-bone had been broken and, in mournful procession, he was taken off by stretcher towards the dressing-rooms.

One shoulder charge, and it made the Final a mockery of a match. Jack Blanchflower moved from centre-half into goal, where he gave a display of which any top-class goalkeeper would have been proud. Worst of all, the young champions lost the power and thrust of Duncan Edwards bursting through at left-half, for he was relegated to the policeman's role at centre-half. Billy Whelan, schemer of the forward line, had to drop back to left-half; where he too played a game that staggered even his most fervent admirers. He looked the best half-back on the field.

That Final lives in the memory for the superb match-winning play of Ireland's Peter McParland; and the poise and class that Manchester United showed with only ten men.

Ten men can and often do beat eleven others – but at Wembley, on that vast pitch against first-class opposition, it is a terrible task. One might just as well expect Sebastian Coe to beat Steve Ovett in a mile race with a pulled muscle; the singles champion at Wimbledon to play the No. 2 when he was not quite on the top line; Ian Botham to score 100 off Bob Willis when he wasn't seeing the ball clearly. In the highest class of sport, only peak form and peak fitness is good enough.

True, in the 1959 Cup Final, ten Nottingham Forest men took the Cup against Luton; but let's not forget the Forest were already two goals up when they lost Dwight, their right-winger, shortly before half-time. Even then their sadly depleted side just managed to hold on for some fifty-five minutes. In Manchester United's case they had to fight level pegging for eighty-four murderous minutes. There was naught they could do but try to play the methodical football which had brought them such wondrous success. Time and time again lovely flowing moves broke down simply because they were a man short.

The brave Wood came back on the field just before half-time to run like a hare along the right touchline. Thousands moaned afterwards that Busby had boobed by not bringing Ray Wood back into his goal until the dying moments of the match when all was lost. The crowd could not – did not – know that under the terraces at Wembley Ted Dalton, the United physiotherapist, had tried shooting a ball at Wood; and the player couldn't even focus his eyes to grab even the simplest of shots. More important, what manager would shove a man with a broken jaw into goal, where the slightest charge, the simplest mêlée, the slightest knock as he went up to gather a ball, could easily have caused Wood a most dangerous injury?

It was the player himself, anxious to assist his mates, who insisted on going back on to the field. If the ball came near him, he could kick it; he could also run after it when he wasn't challenged by a Villa defender. That's all.

Villa, playing the type of football the occasion demanded, won well. They struck soon after half-time with another thunderbolt from McParland. The Irish left-winger, by scoring two goals in a Cup Final, emphasised his right to be called one of the greatest matchwinners in the game. All other goalscoring efforts Blanchflower kept out with a superb display that shook all those who didn't know Jackie was always between the sticks in scratch matches at Old Trafford. Here was a player who could easily have been a top-class goalkeeper, had he not been an even better player as a half-back. It was there that Manchester United needed him most. As the game dragged along, United tried that late switch: Byrne waved Wood back into goal;

Blanchflower went back to centre-half; Edwards, rumbustious, indefatigable, moved to left-half – with some five minutes to go. And what a five minutes, with Edwards surging through like a man who couldn't believe defeat was coming to the champs. He raced madly upfield, taking throw-ins at lightning speed, as Villa lost their grip. Tommy Taylor, shackled by Jimmy Dugdale, suddenly found the form for the occasion.

Duncan Edwards brushed everyone imperiously aside to take a corner on the left. He hit the ball like a bullet, some ten yards out from goal; Tommy Taylor, with a jack-knife leap, beat Dugdale for about the only time in the match, and Villa's lead was cut to 2–1, with only three minutes left. Not enough even for the champs. They stood, in their white shirts with the red edging round the cuffs and collars, beaten but not disgraced, clapping and cheering the Villa men who had brought off the impossible, as they went up to the Royal box to receive the Cup from Her Majesty the Queen. United's fans went home mournfully moaning: 'This would never have happened but for the injury to Wood.'

I don't think it would either. But Villa won the Cup, deservedly, on the day; and in so doing robbed Manchester United of the fabulous double, Cup and League.

Some hours after the match, little Eddie Colman, sipping a lemonade, whispered to me: 'That's football, Frank. Never mind, we are good enough to come to Wembley again next year for the Cup.'

Incredibly, United did. Alas, little Eddie and several of his pals didn't.

14 Last Match in Belgrade

Just before football began again in August 1957, Matt Busby took his team to Berlin and Hanover. The aim: to get the boys warmed up for their assault on the League, FA Cup and European Cup.

Busby told me: 'We must have a chance for all three. But my big aim is to make it a hat-trick of League title wins, just like the great Arsenal side did in the 1930s, and the Huddersfield Town team did in the 1920s.' Both of those sides were made by the greatest manager before Busby, the late Herbert Chapman.

Yet, even if the Munich Air Crash had never happened, I doubt whether Busby's team would have taken the League that season.

Maybe these young players had sampled too much success too early. Perhaps they thought it would be too easy; that the other teams would be beaten before the game by the magical name of Manchester United. British footballers don't think that way. Each and every game the champs played was like a cup tie. Each and every team were determined to knock these cocky youngsters off their perch.

Frisky Eddie Colman, with that maddening body swerve, lost his touch and was dropped. Jack Blanchflower at centre-half lost his command; in goal, Ray Wood had one of those spells which come to every goalkeeper, when every slip costs a goal. The champs were struggling at the start of the season, and the fans at Old Trafford, brought up on a tidal wave of success, were not slow in telling Busby his job. At first he did nothing, but waited for the lads to find their form. Then he acted. At their best, it was impossible to put a cigarette paper between Blanchflower and Mark Jones. Over the years each had shouldered the other out of the first team. It kept both on their toes, and now it was Mark Jones's turn to get back into the big-time. Eddie Colman, after a spell in the reserves, brightened up;

Bill Whelan, the ball juggler, lost his place and the cannonball-shooting Bobby Charlton became first choice. The champions were now hot-foot on the trail of the wonderful Wolves, who had revved up into a big lead at the top of the table from the very start.

Over the years Stan Cullis, one-time England centre-half – and a very classy one at that – had built a powerhouse team as manager of Wolves. They played at a thrilling rip-roaring speed; tackled hard and fairly and their forwards shot with the accuracy of a Bisley marksman. Only a Manchester United team on top form could hope to hold them.

In December 1957 Busby made one of his rare plunges into the transfer market to pay £23,000 for Harry Gregg, the Doncaster Rovers Irish international goalkeeper.

The first match he played, Roger Byrne told him: 'If you come out of goal, Harry . . . you come and knock us out of the way if you have to! We must have no more messing about in the penalty area.'

After the game, I took Harry to the BBC television studios and he declared with an impish Irish grin: 'I've never seen anything like that. When yon wee fellow Colman had the ball and swayed, I swear he made the girders in the grandstand sway when he did.'

With Gregg in goal, United gradually got the results. Matt Busby perked up after the sorry start to the season. 'If we can only close that gap between Wolves and ourselves just after Christmas to three or four points,' he told me, 'I feel sure we'll beat them in the last sprint for the title. There's nobody pushing them just now.'

In the European Cup Manchester United were making heavy weather of their commitments. They went first to Dublin to play Shamrock Rovers. Play? It was a soccer slaughter on Dublin's famed Dalymount Park, as the Shamrock boys wilted to a 6–0 defeat. Billy Whelan took this occasion to show his pals in Dublin that he really could play football. Billy – or Liam, to give him his proper name – dazzled English football crowds with his jinking runs and incredible manipulation of the ball. And though he was capped regularly for Eire, his own countrymen steadfastly refused to believe the local boy was really as good as the English said he was. Dalymount Park,

September 1957, changed all that. Liam was like an Irish leprechaun going through the Irish defenders on twinkling feet that caused the sporting crowd to cheer 'Good old Ireland' even though Whelan the Irishman was systematically decimating his own country's champions.

The crowds teeming into Old Trafford a few weeks later tut-tutted at the slaughter of the Irish innocents which was sure to follow. A score of 6–0 in Dublin was certain to be doubled on Manchester United's own ground. Not so. The soccer certs nearly came unstuck, for the Irish players, if they couldn't match England's proud champions for skill, had outsize hearts under their green jerseys. They made a mockery of football form by holding the Manchester men to 3–2 – and some said United were a shade lucky at that.

The next challengers came from behind the Iron Curtain – Dukla of Prague, champions of Czechoslovakia. They were an Army side and played well-drilled football; defence in depth, neat and tidy – well-planned football which had Byrne and his team-mates struggling to find a way through to Dukla's goal. They took the first leg at 3–0, and everyone from Busby down knew there was going to be one hell of a fight in the return at the Army Stadium in Prague.

That's the way it turned out. Prague was chill and dank in December as they took the Englishmen to the hills overlooking this splendid city to show us a group of five sports arenas. The largest one was capable of holding some 200,000 spectators. On such a ground, the playing pitch looked like a tiny dot in the Red Army Square; with the crowd so far away that one would have needed binoculars to pick up the play. United's men groaned when they saw this vast playing area, but were cheered considerably when they were told the match would be taking place on the much more compact Army stadium. The terraces were lined by khaki-clad figures so that one felt this was more like a day at the Army manoeuvres than a football match. There were Army people everywhere. World-famous athlete Lt-Col Emil Zatopek of the Czech Army sent his apologies for absence, because he was on leave. The fabulous Zatopek, who pumped his way round the world's running tracks breaking records with ridiculous ease on the way, was sorry to miss this soccer show. In this array of Army talent he missed the most splendid display of all, from a shy English corporal called Eddie Colman. The little fellow, all smiles and cheeky football tricks, took Prague by storm. Sure-footed as a mountain goat on a tricky pitch, he and Tommy Taylor were the inspirations of a United team, at times outplayed but who nevertheless managed to keep the Dukla score down to 1 goal – they might have lost more easily. On aggregate, however, they were through at 3–1. United still hadn't found their golden touch; but the signs of a fight back were there.

Fogs over England prevented the touring party picking up their BEA Viscount to fly back to England on the Thursday. The players – after hasty re-planning – were re-routed by Dutch Airlines to Amsterdam and thence to England. The Press boys had to wait till Friday to fly out via Zürich to Birmingham and then to Manchester.

This problem of playing mid-week European Cup matches deep in the heart of the continent, and then making travel arrangements to get the team back to fulfil their English Football League fixtures by the Saturday, was an ever-present headache for Busby and his aides. Failure to honour their League engagement with their strongest available side would have resulted in a heavy fine for the club, and possibly much more violent repercussion with the all-powerful Football League itself. It was this scare in Prague, when the team was almost stranded through fog which kept aircraft grounded, that caused Busby and the club secretary, Mr Walter Crickmer, to make plans for a charter plane on the next European Cup assignment against Red Star, Belgrade, scheduled for the following February.

But first there was an FA Cup hurdle to be cleared at Workington, high up on the Cumberland coast. This little team managed by Joe Harvey, who had twice captained Newcastle United in the Wembley Cup Finals of 1951 and 1952, had scant regard for the ballyhooed Busby team. On a skiddy pitch, they swept eagerly into action. Quite early in the first half Roger Byrne essayed a short back pass to Mark Jones. On that bumpy pitch the ball bounced wildly before it got to Jones and in a trice Ted Purdon, the Workington centre-forward, was racing through the wide-open middle of the field. Harry Gregg advanced from his goal to prevent disaster, but Purdon pushed the ball out to outside-left Clive Collbridge, and United were a goal down and struggling like a team of tenth-raters.

Dennis Viollet took a grip on the game. Small and sure-footed, he swept in three goals in a dynamic burst of power-play in the second half. United were still on the Wembley trail – but this looked anything but the form of a team which still cherished hopes of the League title; which were still strong favourites for the FA Cup; which still hoped for big things in the European Cup.

Suddenly, as so often happens in football, the whole team started to glide from success to success with the precision of a well-oiled machine. Red Star came to Old Trafford and went back to Belgrade losers by 2–1. They brought with them an amazing little inside-forward called Secularac, who was talked of as another continental master-player like the Hungarian Puskas. Quite early in the match he opened his bumper box of football tricks, to cause the crowd shudders whenever he had the ball. Then he was misguided enough to rob Duncan Edwards of the ball, as the muscular left-half was sprinting through. Like a wild buffalo robbed of his prey Edwards turned in a flash, and sprinted like fury after Secularac, and with a thundering tackle whipped the ball away and in his powerful thrust came quite fairly into contact with the little Yugoslav. When Secularac finished his cartwheeling on the turf he was in no fit state to challenge Edwards's possession of the ball; nor in fact did he do much more in the match. Proof, indeed, that at that time the master footballers of Europe were only master footballers until they faced strong, powerful and fair tackling. They were not so used as our men to this style of play. From that point it was United's match. They won 2–1, but they should have had three or four more goals. Beara, the Black Cat in the Yugoslav goal, kept the score down. And as the fans left for home they were just a trifle sad. United's one goal advantage had been narrow enough to see them through against the Dukla side from Prague. Would it be enough in Belgrade? Many football followers thought it wouldn't.

Fog, cold, miserable and depressing, swirled round Ringway Airport on Monday morning, February 3rd, 1958, so that there were grave doubts at first whether the Elizabethan airliner would ever be allowed to take off for Belgrade.

Soon after eight o'clock the mists lifted and we flew off southwards out over the Channel and deep into Germany. To Munich. It was cold and wet as we huddled together in the airport lounge, watching the ground crews refuel the airliner. I stood with Henry Rose and George Follows looking out of the large plate-glass windows at a forbidding wintry scene. Then we grabbed hold of Matt Busby, looking far from well, to find out whether Roger Byrne, who had pulled a thigh muscle, would be fit to play.

The whole party were chatting excitedly about Saturday's game against Arsenal at Highbury just two days previously. On the morning of that match, one of United's directors, eighty-year-old Mr George Whittaker, had died at the London hotel where the team were staying. Some of the players were to act as pall-bearers at the old sportsman's funeral. But that game against Arsenal had put the players in high heart. Leading 3–0 with precision soccer; a sudden slump and it was 4–4. Then they picked up as contemptuously as they had begun, trickling the ball elegantly around the field until even the mighty Arsenal side had folded up 5–4. That was the sort of super soccer they were hoping to turn on in Belgrade – only for a full ninety minutes and not in patches as at Highbury.

Byrne was the one doubt. No one disputed his masterful inspiration as a captain; his uncanny reading of a game; his ability to plan the tactics. And when we interviewed Matt Busby at Munich, he assured us there was good news. It looked as though Byrne would be fit to take his place in United's strongest side after all.

We took off from Munich, and flew on the last leg to Belgrade where there was snow in the streets, but intermittent bursts of spring sunshine. The hotel was like a hothouse with its central heating; but we were much taken by the view from the rear of the hotel, on the patio looking out, as the Danube wound sluggishly along. As usual Matt Busby, Tom Curry, the trainer, and Bert Whalley, the coach, took great care that the players were given English-style food; and nothing highly seasoned which could easily give them 'Gyppo' tummy before the game. The players relaxed, Frank Swift keeping them in high spirits with his own brand of schoolboy pranks. Eddie Colman and Bill Whelan did their celebrated impersonation of a South American

rumba team, with Eric Thompson clacking his fingers for
castanets. All light-hearted and gay. Underneath, the players,
after their recent run of ten matches without defeat, their rip-
roaring crowd-thrilling display against Highbury, desperately
wanted to prove that at long last they were on the victory trail.
They were sure they could win through over these talented
Yugoslav footballers. And beyond that, on the Saturday, there
loomed a more than vital League match with Wolverhampton
Wanderers at Old Trafford. Wolves had been running away in
the title race. Now United, in this recent spell, had pegged their
lead back to four points. A win over them in this next game and
the lead would be a paltry two points. United were geared for
the assault on the League Championship – they meant to make it
a hat-trick of wins if they possibly could. These young
sportsmen made no brash promises; but deep down they were
smarting because Wolves had had the temerity to knock them
from their perch, only too eager to take the title of England's
No. 1 team away from Old Trafford.

Duncan Edwards put the players' view as usual with forceful
forthrightness. 'Let's get this Red Star side out of the European
Cup first, and then we'll deal with Wolves. All I'll say is, that if
the boys play like they did against Arsenal, Stan Cullis's boys
will need to go some to beat us.'

The training pitch in Belgrade looked as though it had been a
swamp recently drained. The Press party and the air crew; the
pilots, Captain Thain and Captain Rayment; the stewardesses,
Miss Bellis and Miss Cheverton; Radio Officer Rogers and the
biggest soccer fan of them all, Steward Tommy Cable, watched
the United players splish-splosh their way round the waterlogged track. They were much taken with Tommy Taylor's
high-stepping graceful run; and they wondered why Roger
Byrne after an electrifying burst of speed should suddenly give
the thumbs-up sign to trainer Tom Curry.

We Press lads knew that Roger had signalled he was definitely
OK to play.

The stadium where the match was to be played was nearby, so
the players showered and trooped off to study the pitch
conditions. It was dusted with a layer of snow and thin ice.
Underneath the turf was firm. If there was no more frost or
snow, playing conditions would be good.

The Wednesday dawned crisp and clear, and the hotel lounge was like a rally of autograph-hunters. Belgrade was afire for the match. The coach taking the players to the ground passed the thousands wending their way to the stadium, chanting and singing and roaring and shouting: 'Busby Babes . . . Busby Babes . . . Red Devils . . . good', as they caught sight of the players. The terraces seethed and rolled in feverish excitement – and then the game was under way. In two minutes flat United were a goal up. It happened like this. A raid on their goal was cleared up-field for Tommy Taylor to chase back, as he so often did, to gather such a clearance. Then the big fellow was off with the Red Star defence spreadeagled. The Belgrade fans couldn't believe their eyes as Big Tommy, moving with grace and power, held on to the ball with Dennis Viollet running alongside his pal.

Everyone expected Taylor to shoot, but with a sudden spurt and swerve he left the defence flat-footed and shoved the ball for Viollet to race on alone unchallenged. Viollet does not miss many chances like that. Ever so carefully he steered the ball past the advancing Beara.

Then the balloon went up. The Belgrade fans erupted into white-hot excitement. On the pitch Ken Morgans, just eighteen, a young player of high promise, had his right thigh ripped open by an over-zealous tackle. Eleven young men kept their heads in this bedlam. They pushed and stroked the ball man to man, making the Red Star players twist and turn and lose their poise. In twenty minutes Bobby Charlton finished another oh so lovely passing move with a thunderbolt shot – and now it was 2–0. Belgrade was rocked . . . Even more rocked when Charlton went racing through yet again. Out of his goal came the acrobatic Mr Beara in his black jersey, to be shattered by a pile-driving shot which hurtled from Charlton's boot well outside the penalty area by some twenty-five yards – to thud into the back of the net. Belgrade couldn't believe it. No one ever shot from so far out and beat Beara. But Charlton did, and England's champions had the game in a stranglehold 3–0 in front. Just on half-time Charlton had the ball in the net again from a corner. He was not the only one surprised when he was given offside.

In all this super football Eddie Colman played with

consummate ease and mobility, which even he had never surpassed. He was always at his best when United were attacking, playing like a sixth forward, wriggling his way through all opposition, probing and pushing for weaknesses, linking up in passing moves of infinite variety, for when the game was fluid and fast, as it was here, then the mobile Colman was great.

The small English contingent in the crowd were overjoyed as their country's champions trotted in at half-time leading by three goals, although everyone admitted they should have had four or even five. That's how good they were.

Henry Rose, in his Press-box seat next to mine, leaned over confidentially. 'Written up, Taylor? The way this is going we can all start writing now.'

Frank Swift shifted his huge frame and turned round. 'You're right Henry – if the lads don't get too cocky and take it too easily.'

Two minutes after the break Secularac floated a surprise shot from outside the penalty area over Harry Gregg's outstretched hands – and it was 3–1. While United took a breather and tried to marshal a defensive game, the Red Stars became shooting stars; the fumbling footballers of the first half now emerged as players of the highest quality, with this little genius Secularac prompting and launching attack after attack.

The strong men in the team, Billy Foulkes and Mark Jones, now fought like furies. Mark Jones, dour and determined Yorkshireman, stopped the flood tide in the middle of the field. Time and time again that blond bobbing head rose above all others, casually to nod the ball clear. Or else his powerful physique and powerful legs were launched in some daring tackle. Alongside him, Billy Foulkes, never a footballer to seek the limelight, didn't put a foot wrong. This was the sort of back-to-the-wall struggle he loved. United's forward line, it seemed, had disintegrated; Duncan Edwards strove powerfully to exert his influence on the game. He was very good; but this was one match where he took second place to the stout-hearted Jones and Foulkes. At left-back Roger Byrne was having a tough time to hold the surging Kapitulski – but Byrne marshalled that defence as though he were a general. Once more the indefatigable Roger waved his arms, extolling his team-mates to greater efforts; pulling his men to cover and hold these non-stop attacks.

Just when they appeared to be holding the fury of this storm, Billy Foulkes raced across to challenge Zebec. He took the ball with one lunge of his boot, and in sliding forward fell to the ground. The ball had gone; there was no danger, but Zebec, enthusiastically following up, fell over the prone Foulkes – who lay there unbelievingly as the referee pointed to the penalty spot.

BANG. That penalty zinged home and now Red Star were trailing 3–2. Behind Harry Gregg's goal the crowd rocked and swayed until several hundreds of them came tippling down the terraces, a tangled mass of human bodies falling down and over the barrier on to the playing pitch itself.

The furious pace was never slackened, and as England's champions tried to find their flowing attacking play of the first half, they were pelted by a storm of snowballs. Two minutes from time Harry Gregg came racing out of his goal, and hurled himself full length at Zebec's feet. He grasped it safely, but the impetus of his rush took him outside the penalty area with the ball, and the Red Star had a free kick some twenty yards out. Kostic watched Gregg position himself by the far post protected by a wall of United players. There was just a narrow ray of light, a gap, by the near post, and precision player Kostic threaded the ball through as Gregg catapulted himself across his goal. Too late, Harry. The ball eluded his grasping fingers, and plonked into the back of the net. The score was 3–3.

Frank Swift turned to me to say: 'What a shame. Harry has had a wonderful game. But he should have stood at the near post and let Kostic shoot for the far post. The ball has longer to travel – and Harry would have longer to see it in its flight.'

It was the last goalkeeping tip I ever heard from Frank Swift, for by now the final whistle had gone and the weary Red Devils trooped off the field. A 3–3 draw put them into the next round of the European Cup, for that 2–1 home win had put them through on aggregate. In the dressing-rooms the players relaxed, grinning.

Roger Byrne paused thoughtfully. 'Football is a funny game, isn't it? I thought we were going to walk it after taking a three-goal lead – but it just shows you can't give these continental sides an inch. Once they get a goal they play like demons. Never mind, we are through to the semi-finals, Frank . . .'

Roger never made that semi-final in Milan, nor did many of his pals. That match in Belgrade when we saw soccer of sublime ease and artistry in the first half, and an unforgettable fight in the second, was the last time anyone saw this wonder side play.

For evermore football followers will be wondering just how great this young team would have become. They had come a long way; and they were still improving. I have no doubts. They would have been the greatest club side ever gathered in England. In fact, when they perished, many people in football thought they were *even then* the greatest ever.

Next morning we flew out from Belgrade for a refuelling stop at Munich. And for Roger Byrne, Duncan Edwards, Tommy Taylor, David Pegg, Bill Whelan, Mark Jones, Eddie Colman and Geoff Bent – the end of the road was to be MUNICH.

15   The Boy Who Had the Lot

Doctor Graham Taylor, of British European Airways, looked rather more serious than usual when he walked in to see Jack Blanchflower and myself on the morning of February 26th, 1958. Normally the Doc, a lithe springy figure, came bounding in, cracking jokes and doing all he could to bring cheer into the place.

'Now then, chaps, how are you today?' The Doc was doing his best to put on his usual air of high good humour. 'Have you any complaints? Is there anything you want? Anything we can do to make you more comfortable?'

When you are lying in bed plastered as we were, there is nothing much you want – except a speedy return to full health.

The Doc chatted about this and that, for a few minutes. He even asked me to do my usual party piece. 'How does Fred Trueman hold the ball for his outswinger?'

The Doc always found this riotously funny, to watch a chap in plaster going through the motions of fearsome Freddie about to unleash a thunderbolt in a Test match.

'I don't think it will be long before Professor Maurer sets Jackie's arm, and has a go at your leg and arm,' he said breezily. But it was obvious something was on his mind. He walked quickly to the door and opened it; turned while still holding the handle and remarked as casually as he could: 'I'm afraid I have some bad news for you both. I know you'll understand, but Duncan couldn't quite make it. He died early this morning. I know you won't tell Matt Busby this sad news. He is too ill to be told yet.'

The news sank in numbly. Duncan Edwards, just twenty-one years of age, the greatest footballer of his generation, had died in the Rechts der Isar Hospital; just twenty-one days after he had played his last game of football in Belgrade. For the last twenty days that powerful body had lain crushed, but the stupendous spirit kept Duncan Edwards going. The world had followed every communiqué of Duncan's twenty days' fight following the crash. But the Big Fellow who feared nothing on a football field had no chance. His injuries were too severe.

He fought with all the unforgettable fury of that unconquerable spirit. And when he died a great sigh went round the sports fields. It was as though a young Colossus had been taken from our midst.

Yet, when the tears were dried, one of Duncan's nearest and dearest friends told me: 'Maybe it was better this way. The doctors said, had he lived, he might have had to spend the rest of his life in a wheelchair. Duncan couldn't have stood that. *Now I can remember him as he was – the greatest thing that has happened in British football for years.*'

The Germans, in their superhuman efforts to keep him going, flew a kidney machine from Stuttgart to Munich. And when it was over, one of those surgeons who had been at his bedside for hours on end said: 'I have seen death many, many times – but never like this. In all my years, I have never seen a whole hospital staff so upset. This boy we have never seen before, he comes to our hospital – but he is so young, so strong . . . so brave. *Ach*, but he had no chance.'

So young . . . so strong . . . so brave. Those of us who knew Duncan, who saw him burst across the football firmament like a meteor, would expect such an epitaph. In five and a half years he became a legend in his own lifetime; a young Hercules.

Who can doubt that, had he lived, Duncan would have broken Bobby Moore's record of playing 108 times for England?

Just a month before the Munich crash, while discussing an article with Matt Busby, the latter remarked: 'I rate Duncan Edwards the most Complete Footballer in Britain – if not the world.'

I knew what Busby meant. He carefully chose those words 'Complete Footballer', for only recently the Italian Club Juventus had paid out some £75,000 to buy John Charles from Leeds United.

Charles, the marvellous Welshman, bigger than Duncan Edwards, more deadly in the air; and you could argue, quite rightly, he had better ball control than Edwards. The difference was this. Charles was called Gentle John, the genial giant. Duncan Edwards was genial off the field. On it, he knew only one way to play – all out from the first minute to the last. He was stronger than Charles in the tackle; more powerful going through for goal. It was sometimes possible to shut John Charles out of a game; Duncan Edwards never. He never held back from a tackle; he never gave up trying; he was always in the game, always looking for the ball. Charles often played in spasms. Edwards had only one style, whether it was a junior match or for England – 100 per cent Go all the time. As a wing-half he could play like a sixth forward going through to score. He could also on instructions play the shadow man, scarcely venturing over the halfway line. As a wing-half John Charles was never as dominant as that.

Duncan's favourite position was left-half, for he was always in the game there. But he could, and did, play centre-half, centre-forward and inside-forward, and he could mould his play no matter what the position exactly on the lines he was told to, whether by Matt Busby for Manchester United or Walter Winterbottom for England.

I have seen Duncan Edwards hooted and booed at by thousands of irate Scots thundering from the terraces at Hampden Park.

I have seen Duncan Edwards cheered and fêted in Madrid, in Berlin, and in London. It made no difference. He played football because he loved football. The cheers or jeers mattered not at all. He got his big kick from the game itself.

This was the boy who died at Munich, although you might say he was never a boy – he was old beyond his years as a footballer. A human dynamo built on gargantuan lines. Even as a schoolboy he played a man's-type game first with his cousin Dennis Stevens, the Bolton Wanderers' inside-left, then for Dudley, and then for England Boys. A dozen First Division clubs would have liked to sign Edwards, but it was the old firm of Matt Busby and Jimmy Murphy who took him to Old Trafford.

So far as I am concerned, Duncan Edwards was first introduced to the wider sporting public in an article which came from the magic pen of George Follows. He had a tip-off that Duncan would soon be appearing for Manchester United, although not yet sixteen, as the latest of the Busby Babes. Follows, good newspaperman that he was, wrote a delightful piece in the northern editions of the *News Chronicle* about 'The Boy Who Had the Lot'.

Johnny Carey stated Duncan was the greatest player at his age he had ever seen.

Jack Rowley, of the thunderbolt shot, said of young Edwards: 'I wish I could hit a ball like Duncan. Thirty, forty yards. Makes no difference. He hits them like a bomb.'

Duncan Edwards played for Manchester United against Cardiff City at Old Trafford, Easter Monday 1953. He was just fifteen years and 285 days. It was his first game in the First Division. I saw it, just as I saw his last game in Belgrade.

I wish I could say I was an Edwards fan from the very beginning. In fact, I was at first just a little sceptical. As I got back to the Manchester offices of the *News Chronicle*, George Follows eagerly quizzed me. 'What's your verdict, Frank?'

'Looks a wonderful prospect; tackles well; hits a lovely long ball – but he looks a bit thick round the hips. He'll need to train to keep his weight down,' I replied.

This snap verdict was proved complete nonsense, and illustrates the snags of a quick assessment of a player's ability.

At the time of Munich, Duncan Edwards had proved George Follows right all along the line. He did have the lot. He was not too heavy as I predicted he might be. He was fast and very fit. He got rid of that puppy fat because he trained like a maniac. He was what Matt Busby claimed him to be: 'The most Complete Footballer in Britain – perhaps the world.'

Duncan came from Dudley, which is almost within shouting distance of Wolverhampton. Why then did he go to Manchester and not that other great team, Wolverhampton Wanderers?

Duncan always sidestepped that query with a disarming smile. 'I was always a Manchester United fan when I saw what a great team Mr Busby built after the war. I always wanted to join them,' he said.

Now look what the Wolves missed when Edwards preferred Old Trafford to Molineux.

1. Youngest ever professional to play in the First Division when he appeared for Manchester United at Old Trafford

against Cardiff City at the tender age of fifteen years and 285 days, in April 1953.

2. Youngest ever footballer to play for England in a full international. He was 17 years and 8 months when he played for England against Scotland at Wembley, April 1955. England won 7–2.

3. He captained England Schoolboys, and the Under-23's, and was tipped to take over Billy Wright's mantle as England's skipper in the years to come.

4. He had nineteen full caps for his country.

5. He won two League Championship medals with Manchester United in 1956 and 1957.

6. He gained an FA Cup runners-up medal when Manchester United lost 2–1 to Aston Villa in the 1957 Final at Wembley.

Just where do you stop? He had played in the European Cup semi-final; played all over the continent with his country and his club; and had won every honour available to him, except a Cup-winner's medal and a Second Division Championship medal. It is hard to visualise him adding the last distinction to his collection.

He was one on his own. Crowds and criticisms left him unmoved, or, like the true champion he was, he hid his true feelings under a mask of indifference.

Crowds? Come back with me to Hampden Park, April 1956. The Scottish fans had heard a great deal about the new dreadnought Duncan Edwards. Now he was to play before that critical crowd for the first time in a full international and Duncan had the tough task of shutting that bubbling genius Bobby Johnstone out of the game.

Within the opening minutes the Scottish forwards tried a smart forward shuffle, which left the mercurial Johnstone darting like an arrow from inside-right to the left-wing touchline. Who could imagine that a young beginner like Edwards could follow so bewildering a move so early in an international? As Johnstone's tiny figure moved like quicksilver for the ball so too did Edwards. The charge of the Heavy Brigade against the Light. It was a fair tackle and it was a heavy tackle. They lifted the diminutive Johnstone reverently and slowly back on to the pitch. Edwards? He shook himself like a frisky puppy, then stood up. It was not surprising that thereafter Bobby Johnstone did not have one of his greatest games.

It was not surprising either that Edwards was roundly booed every time he went near the ball. It did not disturb him. The louder the Scots booed, the better he played. He had a job of work to do for England; and he did it brilliantly.

And Johnstone? Ask Bobby now, and he will tell you without hesitation: *'Duncan Edwards was the greatest footballer I ever saw or played against.'*

Criticisms? Duncan's hairy-chested approach to the game frequently brought the quite wrong accusation that he was a dirty player. Not true. He was never a dirty player. His tough, he-man approach to sport once caused my friend Henry Rose to open up a broadside against Duncan in the *Daily Express*. He did it by writing an open letter – read by millions of *Express* readers – urging the lad to curb his exuberant approach to the game. 'Don't be a toughie,' pleaded Henry.

After he had published the piece, Henry the peacemaker had second thoughts. Maybe he had been too tough on a young player still in the early years of his career. When next he went to Old Trafford, Henry pushed his way down to the dressing-rooms under the stands, and buttonholed Duncan.

'Hope you didn't mind my public censure of your play in the *Express*,' Henry began. 'Don't let it put you off your game, son. But people are talking, and I don't want to see you get a bad name in the game, as a chap who puts brawn before brains.'

Duncan beamed boyishly. 'Never even read it, Henry, so it doesn't hurt me. I don't mind what the papers say about me. After all, you have a job of work to do. You must justify your pay. That's fair enough by me. I don't really care what you write about me. It's what Mr Busby says that I take notice of . . . But it's very kind of you to think of me that way.'

This brash reply flabbergasted the usually ebullient Henry. 'Can you beat that?' he said afterwards. 'No player ever spoke that way to me before.' And in his warm-hearted way, Henry smiled: 'But you have to hand it to the kid though. I don't believe he does care what the Press says about him.'

Cheers? Duncan accepted those as part of a footballer's life – like the jeers. 'It's nice to be cheered,' he once told me, 'but you can't live for ever on cheers. It's what you have in the bank when you have finished with the game that cheers a footballer most of all. People forget very easily and I don't want to become like some of the old-timers wearing tattered caps and cadging free tickets outside the grounds.'

With that remark Duncan revealed he knew only too well where he was going in the game. He wasn't going to be a sucker for the cheap applause.

Beneath the mask of the man there was still that streak of shy boyishness. I saw it in Berlin in August 1957. A few months earlier, he had bulldozed the England team into a thrilling 3–1 win over Germany, when from some twenty-five yards he had thrashed in a goal which caused the Germans to christen him 'BOOM BOOM Edwards – the chap with a Big Bertha Shot in his boots'. And they remembered that when Manchester United flew to Berlin in August 1957 for a short pre-season tour. As our plane touched down at Templehof Airport there was a wild surge of soccer fans, sports writers and cameramen chanting:

'BOOM BOOM. Where is BOOM BOOM Edwards?'

I was coming out of the plane directly behind Duncan. He shied away at the reception.

'Go on. You go first, Frank,' he said. 'Pretend you are me.'

'Don't be daft, Duncan,' I replied. 'They are looking for a sleek athlete. That rules me out.'

Duncan stared at my roly-poly figure. 'Maybe you have something there.' And with that he heaved himself through the hatch and down the steps to the tarmac.

As soon as the crowd spotted him, they darted forward. 'BOOM BOOM. . . . This way please . . . smile . . . a picture, please.'

Edwards tried to brush aside this film-star-style reception as flashlight bulbs popped in his face. 'Get the whole team. Manchester United are a team. You want the other chaps too.'

As Duncan tried to hide his face, Roger Byrne, smirking all over his face at the big fellow's discomfiture, said: 'Go on, Boom Boom. Smile. Watch the Birdie.'

The cameramen had now switched their lenses on the entire team. 'Go on, Byrnie, now you watch the Birdie,' quipped Duncan.

Whenever you asked Duncan the secret of Manchester United's astonishing success he would answer cutely: 'Easy. We have the two best managers in the game. Mr Busby and his number 2, Jimmy Murphy.' A sweeping statement from a player who was intensely loyal; who never forgot the leg-pulling he received from Jimmy Murphy when he first went to Old Trafford on the ground staff. As the years rolled on, Duncan and Jimmy never ceased poking fun at one another.

Just four months before the air crash, Murphy and Edwards were in rival football camps: Duncan as England's left-half for the international against Wales, at Ninian Park, Cardiff; while Murphy sat on the sidelines as the Welsh team manager. In his pre-match tactical talk, Murphy ran through the England strengths and weaknesses; where he hoped the Welsh might strike. When he came to the name of Duncan Edwards, he paused for a moment and then said without a smile: 'This fellow Edwards has pretty strong legs, so if you go into a tackle with him – make sure you kick the ball and not his leg. *If you do, you'll break your own!*'

The Welsh team roared. Duncan Edwards's legs were famed throughout football, more like young oak trees than legs! Not many players ever relished going into a full-blooded tackle with him.

In that match England were leading 4–1, with some twenty minutes to go. Jimmy Murphy, who never believes any game is lost until the final whistle blows, sat red of face shouting and urging his team to greater efforts: 'Come on, boys. You can do it. In for that ball now.' Casually Duncan Edwards ran to take a throw-in near where Jimmy sat. 'Aren't there any early trains back to Manchester, Jim? You're wasting your time here,' he chortled.

Jimmy Murphy glowered. 'I'll see you when I get back to Old Trafford, m'lad – just to tell you what you are doing wrong.'

Nobody appreciated Duncan's wisecrack more than Murphy himself. And being the man he is, he never says anything about the agonies of mind he suffered when he saw Duncan Edwards lying so helpless in the Munich hospital, plaintively asking what had happened to the presentation gold watch the Real Madrid club had given him. Or of how they searched the wreckage of the airliner until they found a battered wristwatch, brought it back, and strapped it on Duncan's wrist. That made the big fellow happy. He didn't shout for it any more, he just kept asking Jim Murphy: 'What time is the kick-off against Wolves, Jim? I mustn't miss that game.'

And all the time the German surgeons marvelled at the tremendous spirit of the man; while they worked methodically night and day hoping for the miracle that was not to be.

Although his own son lay so desperately ill, Duncan's father, Mr Gladstone Edwards, never failed to come along each day to see how Jack Blanchflower and myself were progressing. 'How is Duncan?' we would ask. And Mr Edwards, with the air of a man who hopes for the best yet fears the worst, would reply: 'Not too bad, lads – but don't you worry about him. We want to see you up and about again pretty soon.'

Neither Jack Blanchflower nor myself realised then that Duncan was mortally injured. Not until that morning of February 26th when Dr Graham Taylor broke the sorrowful news.

I looked at him now standing by the still-open door, hoping against hope that there had been some terrible mistake. Seven young footballers had perished on the airfield; now Duncan was the eighth. My heart sank in numbing despair: why, I had seen Duncan playing football just a few days before in Belgrade, full of zip and vigour. Not one of his greatest games, but good enough for the little Yugoslavian star Secularac to say to us later:

'This Edwards is very good and so powerful. He will not be beaten; he is maybe the greatest player in the world. I wish he played for us.'

That's what they said about him in Belgrade. Surely he couldn't have slipped away like that? Only too clearly Dr Taylor's face showed the sad news was true.

Overwhelming sorrow swept into the room. If Duncan couldn't make it, what chance did a much older Matt Busby have? What chance did Blanchflower and myself have?

It was inconceivable. Never again would we see that sudden spurt of Edwards, all muscle and strength, as he came running out of the players' tunnel; those wild boyish leaps of sheer exuberance as he ran on to the pitch. Why, it seemed he could never wait for the whistle to blow and the game to get started. Never again to see that matchless physique crashing into thrilling action; a giant of the football world while little more than a boy.

'O God, help his family,' I whispered.

In the bed next to mine black despair creased the usually happy face of Jack Blanchflower. I could see the tears start to roll and I thought he was going to cave in, completely nerve-shaken.

'Stick it, son. We can't help Duncan now. Your wife Jean will be here soon.' I saw Blanchflower bury his head in the bedclothes and turned away to do the same. Words couldn't help.

There were many tears that day in Munich, and far beyond, for a boy who had taken the world of sport by storm; who epitomised the power and zest and all that's best in British sport. A worthy young sports idol for the youth of the nation. Duncan Edwards was unforgettable.

So long, Dunc. It was great while it lasted.

16   Be *Not* Afraid

Professor Maurer held his thumb and forefinger very close together, maybe an eighth of an inch apart. 'It is a little better, Mr Taylor – just a little better.' It was late at night when he called, and he stood in the doorway beaming.

Herr Doktor Oppelt winked behind his chief's back and gave the thumbs-up sign. 'It is much better, Mr Taylor,' he whispered. I went to sleep happy. Looked as though they would save my leg after all.

Next morning the smiles were wiped away. Professor Maurer arrived chirpy as a lark and came to the bedside and gripped my arm. 'OK, Mr Taylor, the infection is better. Now we can operate.'

My life as a sports writer takes me among the fit and the athletic, the young folk and those bubbling with vitality; the players' changing-rooms and the stink of liniment. Sure, I've sat in the dressing-rooms and watched a fighter having his eye stitched. But an operation? I'd never had an operation in my life. I was frightened of being put to sleep, in case I might never wake up again.

Since then, several doctors have explained that this is a natural fear for people having an anaesthetic for the first time. I tell the story now, for maybe it will help others not to be afraid in these days of miracle surgery.

When Professor Maurer told me that despite the weeks of waiting my leg still needed surgery, I was in a blue funk.

I tried to explain to him that I didn't want gas. And could he please do it by local anaesthetic? He roared with laughter. 'This is a skin graft, Mr Taylor. A little skin graft to put over your wounds so . . . and this will help the bones to heal more quickly.'

Panic-stricken I asked: 'But where will you take the skin from?'

The German professor fairly roared. As he was talking to me, a young and pretty woman doctor was leaning over, taking a blood test, and the Professor, as he passed, tapped her lightly on the rump. 'From there, Mr Taylor. But of course. Nothing but the best for you.'

It was his way of making a somewhat shaken patient a little more cheerful. When Dr Frank Preston of BEA came round, I tackled him. 'This skin graft. Is there no chance of having it done by local anaesthetic?'

He grinned cheerfully. 'Good heavens, what are you worried about? A little prick of pentathol, and bingo you're out for a quiet afternoon's snooze. It's as simple as that. Tomorrow night you'll be wondering why on earth you were worried.'

The Doc was right. But at that moment I wished the whole damn' business was over and done with. Perhaps it was as well I didn't know that I had another ten trips like this ahead, and that it would be another eighteen months before I could stand up properly on my own legs again.

The hours dragged like months the first time. They tell me some patients can go to the operating theatre singing and joking; others behave as though their last hour had come. Put me among the latter category – on that first trip anyway. Jack Blanchflower tried to cheer me up; so did my sister Barbara, as she waited. When Sister Gilda came in to wheel me away, my sister gripped my hand. 'I'll be waiting for you when you come back,' she said affectionately.

When I came back? I was sure I wouldn't be coming back! Anxiously I looked at the huddled groups of nurses and doctors in their white masks and theatre boots; the still figures in the beds, as we passed one operating theatre after another; the almost overpowering closeness of the place. Many have made a similar journey. For some silly reason, I recalled a famous phrase of Peter Wilson, the *Daily Mirror* sports columnist. Peter, renowned among ring writers, had a habit of referring to the boxing ring as 'the loneliest place on earth'.

I thought: 'Peter, old boy, you are wrong. The ring isn't the loneliest place; a patient being wheeled into the operating theatre feels an awful lot lonelier. After all, he can't *hit back*!'

I don't suppose there is any one of us who can make that trek without thinking: this could be the last time I'll see the lights again; see people again; see my loved ones again. Suppose the anaesthetist doesn't know his job? If there is a slip? After all, anyone can make mistakes. Even surgeons! What if my heart stops beating and they can't get it going again? And foremost in my mind: what if this skin graft is just an excuse to get me down here? Perhaps they will take my leg off after all.

Don't laugh. A man or a woman facing an operation doesn't always see things with the same logical mind as those who are fit and well.

There is only one Comforter in dire extremity. Suddenly I felt quite content as they pushed me through the doors, for there came flooding into my mind a celebrated broadcast by the late King George VI in wartime, which put great heart into the fighting men. The words?

'I said to the man who stood at the Gate of the Year, give me a light that I may tread forth safely into the Unknown. And he replied, Put your Hand in the Hand of God, that is better than any light and safer than any known way.'

Those were the words as I remembered them. Why all this foolish worry? I had survived the worst blows of the air crash; struggled through a bout of pneumonia and shock; hung on these four weeks while the surgeons cleaned up the worst of the mess. What was difficult about removing a piece of skin? This was progress.

Quite inexplicably I felt a surge of confidence. A graceful figure with fine chiselled features, from which dangled a mask, came over. 'Ah, Mr Taylor. You are my patient. It will not be long.' I looked at the tapered fingers of Frau Doktor Ursula Schmidt, who, like our own world-famed Sir Archibald McIndoe, was a skin-graft specialist. She had nice hands. I hoped they didn't slip.

By this time a small, well-rounded blonde had joined Doktor Schmidt. No one could say the Germans didn't have enough female company to cheer the dithering patient! This small woman doctor had a hypodermic syringe in one hand as she started to examine my right arm, rubbing the veins to make them stand out. 'Now where shall we put this?' she enquired. 'There is not a good collection of veins, is there?'

'They've gone in hiding through fear of that needle,' I replied.

Finally she picked her spot as she still chatted soothingly:

'Now see if you can count to ten in German?' she asked sweetly. I had reached '*fünf*' after the needle had pricked my arm, then my eyelids started to flutter and I couldn't keep them open as my senses started to flee as they had done in the air crash.

'*Gute Nacht*,' I whispered, although it was early afternoon. I didn't hear the reply.

While I was unconscious, Doktor Schmidt worked deftly, removing a strip of skin from my left thigh, and placed it carefully on one of the huge gashes on my right leg. It was a tricky job. The sort of operation many wartime flyers endured at the hands of the great specialist Sir Archibald McIndoe and his team, when they treated the terribly burned cases in air crashes.

In the treatment of severely broken legs which are badly infected, the aim is to transfer this skin, and gradually get the outside flesh to heal and rebuild the broken tissue. Years ago the only answer was amputation. These days, skin grafts can seal off the fractures, and give the bones a chance to unite again. Thus, many thousands who would be limbless are saved by the painstaking skill of the skin-graft experts and the orthopaedic surgeons.

Before they had finished months of treatment, a series of operations had to be performed on my right leg; and each time the skin was taken from the left until it looked like a patchwork quilt. As Professor Maurer remarked with a smile: 'Nature is wonderful. Your left leg is helping to save your right.'

This operation by Frau Doktor Schmidt was the first. But I slept peacefully as her dextrous fingers carefully and methodically planted the new skin on my right shin.

It was six o'clock when I woke, to find my sister at my bedside, my wife having had to fly back to England to see our children safely settled with their grandmother. Faintly across the other side of the room I could see Jack Blanchflower and his wife Jean smiling. 'Ah. He's awake at last.'

Anxiously I felt beneath the bedclothes. Good – my leg was still there. What a chump I had been to worry so much! It was just as Dr Preston had said it would be. A slight prick in the arm and then a snooze like someone falling asleep after lunch.

'Can I have a cup of tea?' I asked my sister.

17 Spring Comes to Munich

Spring came like a long-awaited friend to Southern Germany. First the trees four floors below in the garden shyly pushed their first shoots of green towards the watery sun, which inflamed the faraway snow-capped peaks of the Bavarian Alps until they shimmered with rivers of gold.

A warming sun; not the steam heat of summer, but just warm enough to bring life flowing back into the bodies of the injured still in hospital. Along the verandah, which ran the length of the hospital, patients and staff sunned themselves. Most mornings the surgeons and operating-theatre sisters and orderlies would grab a ten-minute break, sitting in gaily coloured deck-chairs, smoking and talking and drinking tea or coffee, thankfully taking great gulps of fresh air after the stuffy cloying atmosphere of the theatres. Down below the trams clanked along. It was good to be alive. Further along that balcony, Matt Busby, still very weak, waved a hand as he sat in a wheelchair watching a group of small German boys playing football down below on a tiny patch of green grass.

'Seen any likely lads worth a trial at Old Trafford, Matt?' I shouted to him. Matt grinned. He was taking an interest in football again. Practically every day Professor Frank Kessel, the small, compact, fresh-complexioned brain surgeon, came along to see the English patients. A Viennese, he bubbled with vitality. He waltzed rather than walked into the room; gay, cheerful, speaking English with all the natural idiom of a man who had spent ten years of his life as a surgeon at Manchester's Royal Infirmary. The small neat hands were as well formed as a woman's, and they gripped like steel. When he first came into my room I called him politely enough Professor Kessel. After two days of this he smiled jocularly. 'My name is Frank,' he said. 'You are Frank too. From now on it is Frank to Frank.' I was startled at the man's frankness. No professor had spoken to me that way before.

No matter how busy he was, or how tired after precise and arduous operations, he still made time to come and see us – Johnny Berry chiefly, then Matt and myself. He did this, I think, because he spoke English so well and could translate anything that worried us. And also, because he had lived and worked in Manchester, he could talk about places we knew and people he had met.

Whenever I tried to thank him for what the hospital staff had done he brushed it aside with a smile. 'We did nothing. Nothing at all that would not have been done in an English hospital in the same circumstances. Medicine is international, it was our *duty* to do what little we could. You must never forget a great deal depends on the patient – and some of these British boys have been absolutely wonderful. No fuss, no bother, real British phlegm in very difficult circumstances. And you know, Frank, good surgeons can only do their best. After that they must leave their work in the Hands of the Great Healer!'

What could you say to a chap like that? My wife found the best answer. 'Sometimes God calls on quite remarkable people to help Him carry out His work,' she said.

When Manchester United played Fulham in the re-played FA Cup semi-final at Highbury, my colleagues Roy Moor and Pat Collins in the London office of the *News Chronicle* arranged for me to get a ball-by-ball description of the game. This was just the sort of tonic to take one's mind out of the ordinary routine of hospital life. Who should come dashing in, midway through the afternoon after finishing an operation, but Professor Kessel. 'Is our team winning?' he called with a mischievous grin. He always classed himself humorously as the president of the Manchester United Supporters' Club – Munich branch! There were only a few minutes left, so he stayed until he heard that United had won through to the Final, and rushed off to tell Professor Maurer and the rest of the hospital staff that Busby's team had achieved the impossible by recovering from the effects of the Munich Air Crash and had reached the Cup Final for the second year in succession.

That news was just the tonic and upsurge Matt Busby needed to push him further along the road to recovery. The question

now on everybody's lips? Would the doctors pass Matt fit
enough to travel back to England to see his club play Bolton
Wanderers at Wembley?

I desperately wanted to go back to see that Cup Final too; to
go to the Football Writers' Dinner; to see all the Press colleagues
again: Bill Hicks, John Camkin, Ian Wooldridge, Frank Butler,
Harry Ditton, Des Hackett, Bob Pennington, Capel Kirby,
Maurice Smith, Edgar Turner, Len Noad, Jack Wood, Roy
Peskett – oh, there was a list as long as your arm. Wouldn't it be
great to be among that rip-roaring mob again; to hear the
wisecracks ripped out by Tommy Trinder, Fulham's chairman;
to be back in the hurly-burly of the football world again just
twelve weeks after the crash!

Was that too much to hope for?

I tackled Professor Kessel. 'What's the chances of me being
back for the Cup Final?'

He looked at me seriously, still encased in plaster from neck to
toe. 'Wouldn't it be nice to see your friends again, Frank?' he
began. 'But, young man,' he paused a moment, pointing to the
sky, 'each and every day you should thank Him above who
ordained where you sat in that aeroplane.'

That's all the Professor said. I knew I wouldn't be going to
Wembley even if Matt did.

The sun grew stronger as the days passed deep into April. The
snowstorms of February were now an occasional and unpleasant
memory. Spring was bursting out all over, and even if I couldn't
go to Wembley to see the Cup Final, the doctors did relent a
little. They said I could go down in a wheelchair and sit in the
garden. After the weeks in one room it was like a reprieve for a
prisoner doomed to solitary confinement.

On that happy day, Father Angelo O'Hagan, an Australian
Franciscan monk, came in to see me. He came to all the injured
immediately after the accident, a tall well-built Australian of the
Outdoors Keith Miller breed. When I told him I was not a
Catholic, he tossed it off with a laugh. 'I don't care what you are.
But if you would like me to come in to talk sport with you . . . I'd
be happy to do so.' He did just that for twenty-one weeks, three
times a week; a man still under thirty who could converse in
half-a-dozen tongues, and yet still earthy, able to talk on many
diverse subjects – cricket and Rugby League included. Why, he

even jokingly challenged me to a cycle race – when my leg and arm were better.

It was this jovial monk – looking for all the world like someone who had strayed from the Middle Ages into the twentieth century – who came in to see me now. He gazed stunned at the figure in the wheelchair swathed in blankets, a pair of sunglasses perched on the nose in the case the sun was too fierce after the weeks of shelter in hospital and on the top of my head a ridiculous fawn beret which might have looked more appropriate perched on Bobby Locke's head in the Open Golf Championship.

'Going golfing, Francis?' said Father Angelo. He always noted with glee my discomfiture at being hailed as Francis instead of Frank. He came into the lift with Sister Gilda and my wife who were taking me out in the wheelchair.

The lift slid silently down four floors and then we were on the ground floor of this extraordinary hospital built in the Middle Ages and now modernised until it was more like a hotel than a hospital. At least the entrance was. Everywhere bright and gay: a counter where the visitors could get flowers for the patients; a cluster of shops where one could buy perfume or sweets, or leather goods or similar presents; a barber shop where the women patients could book for a perm to be done either on the premises or even in their own beds. I leave the reader to imagine what a tremendous boost to the morale this is for women who may have weeks of medical treatment ahead of them. Gay pictures on the walls; plants turned round wrought-ironwork and fishes swimming round in tanks set into the walls. These fleeting impressions hit the eye as I was wheeled out into the green of the gardens and the sunshine. I felt like crying.

The patients, both men and women, were walking and talking quite freely, moving around the grounds clad in dressing-gowns without the slightest trace of shyness. Everywhere was so green, such a lovely lush green; the leaves of the trees starting to arrow their way towards the sun; the first shoots of the flowers by the lawns; the pond and the water-lilies with the ducks waggling along on their spring courtship. Outside the walls the cars and taxis raced by, their horns blaring. Such an infernal racket – but I was back amongst the living again and up there on the fourth balcony Matt Busby looked down on this scene.

My mind somersaulted back to the miserable desolation of snow and slush at Munich Riem Airport and the leaden skies; and then I was back again in the present, admiring this lovely greenery and the crocuses starting to poke through with shafts of blue and yellow.

'O God, why am I seeing all this beauty of spring when my friends perished in the snow?' Then I recalled the words of Professor Kessel: 'Every day you should thank Him above who ordained where you sat in that aeroplane.'

Father Angelo must have seen the conflicting emotions on my face and that I was very close to tears. 'What's wrong, Francis?' he enquired breezily.

'I was just thinking about the other boys,' I said. 'They didn't see spring this year.'

The Father looked back squarely and with great kindness. 'I shouldn't worry. They'll be in a far better place than this.'

I wanted to tell him what great guys they were. The laughs we had had flying across Europe; or in the trains winding around the North as we did our stint reporting football matches, and nearly always the centre of those laughs was Eric Thompson.

Eric, a short dumpy man with perpetually twinkling eyes and fair hair, was known to *Mail* readers as a serious sports writer with an astonishing flair for the funny side of sport which he drew in equally funny sketches.

One of the last games he reported in England was on Sheffield Wednesday's ground, Hillsborough, when he wrote: 'So many centres flashed across M— in goal that it must have looked like a non-stop windscreen wiper to him.' And Eric drew a goalkeeper with the ball flashing backwards and forwards across the goal – just like a windscreen wiper.

He convulsed the Press box when he first saw Duncan Edwards appear in a dandy new red shirt. 'Must be the biggest pillar box ever seen on a football pitch,' quipped Eric.

He silenced a pompous self-opinionated cricket writer who announced in tones of sheer dogma: 'Of course, old chap, the only way to watch a cricket match is right behind the bowler's arm so that you can see what the ball is doing.'

'I tried it once,' replied Eric without the trace of a smile. 'But the umpire made me move my deckchair back. Said I was interfering with the bowler's run up.'

We were not surprised next day to see a Thompson sketch of a spectator being ordered to move his chair which he had placed on the field right behind the bowler's arm some six yards behind the stumps.

In the high-pressure business of searching for sports news Eric Thompson was an enigma. Impeccably dressed, immaculate manners and yet with it all an outrageous sense of fun tilting like a lance at the pompous and self-righteous who clutter the sporting scene. The gags and jokes followed him like a benign cloud with that remarkable sense of mimicry which would make him broad Lancashire one moment, very typically Cockney the next, with, on occasion, a wonderful impersonation of an Italian tenor at a football match.

Eric Thompson I saw spend a contemplative morning in Madrid admiring the paintings and works of art, the architecture and the flaming colours of that city, then he convulsed an entire shop when he was buying presents by picking up some castanets and giving a magnificent burlesque of a narrow-hipped flamenco dancer. That was Eric Thompson, my Press pal, who died in the air crash.

I looked round the gardens of the Rechts der Isar Hospital; at the splash of colour from the flowers; the church steeple just down the road and the glistening white peaks of the Bavarian Alps in the far distance slashed with stripes of pure gold from the rays of the sun.

The artist in Eric Thompson would have loved that scene.

'Come on, let's go back inside,' I said to my wife and Father Angelo.

18   My Press Friends

The people who poured into the Rechts der Isar Hospital in Munich to see Matt Busby and the other injured stepped straight from the Sportsman's Debrett. Messages flowed in from all over the world; Soccer fans hitch-hiked their way across Germany to come and see the manager of Manchester United. And as Busby started to get better, there was a non-stop flow of Pressmen anxious to grab the first interviews.

Everyone wanted to know, would Matt come back to football? Would he be able to build his team again? What was going to be the effect on English Football through the loss of such giants as Duncan Edwards, Roger Byrne, Tommy Taylor?

The results of the England team in the following years gave the answer. The loss of Edwards, Byrne and Taylor was appalling. If I pick out Edwards as the greatest of this great trio, it is merely because only once in a lifetime is such an astonishing collection of football skills crammed into one man.

There was one thing about these visitors who came in, principally to see Busby – they brought laughter back into life.

Ken Wolstenholme, famed BBC television sports commentator, came in several times to see me. He is a friend of long standing and when he saw me encased in plaster, trying to hoist myself up in bed with the aid of a wooden bar, he rocked with laughter.

'Pardon me,' he said, 'I had no idea you were practising as a trapeze artiste – if you improve I'll try and get you a booking at the Palladium.'

As a bomber pilot of some distinction in the war, Ken knew only too well that laughter is the greatest healer of all to a man badly injured.

So too did Des Hackett, the slick sports writer of the *Daily Express*. Des expertly surveyed the plaster cast wrapped round my chest and wrote on it in tiny letters: 'Sir Stanley Rous's secret hideout for Cup Final tickets . . . bring your own pick and shovel to break in here.'

I had to tell Des about the new knock-out specialist I had discovered. Having spent some hours round the ringsides, watching muscular men trying to pound each other into insensibility, I find myself coming round more and more to the opinion of Dr Edith Summerskill. For one thing, there is such an appalling waste of effort. There are much simpler ways of knocking a person out than by throwing punches at the chin.

I said to Des: 'You know, you boxing writers pound out your pieces about the big white hopes and the great black hopes . . . and the chaps with dynamite-laden fists. But there is a wee blonde down the corridor there, with blue eyes and the delicate look of a piece of Dresden china, but she is the greatest knock-out specialist I ever saw. One tiny prick of her pentathol-loaded needle . . . and, brother, you're out stone cold. And you don't get up off the canvas either. She's put me out four times already, and the last time I saw her I apologised: "You have a pretty face, Fräulein, yet every time I see you I fall asleep." "Don't worry, Mr Taylor," she replied, "you're going to sleep again." And I did.'

Des Hackett roared when he heard that yarn. 'Keep it quiet, Frank, or Jack Solomons will be wanting to put that blonde knock-out specialist on his next promotion!

It was the visits of chaps like Des, Ken, Cliff Michelmore and Ronnie Noble of BBC television which made the days whizz past. One day the nurses brought in a matron from England to see me. She had read so much about the Munich hospital, she wanted to see it, to compare it with English hospitals. She was so kind and helpful that I offered to repay her by visiting her hospital when I got back to England, and giving the patients a talk on sport.

She smiled ever so sweetly. 'That is kind of you but I don't think my patients would be very keen on a sports talk, Mr Taylor. Care and feeding of babies would be more in their line. *You see, I'm matron of a maternity hospital.*'

The day that Johnny Carey flew into Munich was one of the funniest of all. To those who have never heard of Johnny Carey – and there must be very few people who haven't – he is a chap with a large and somewhat professorial forehead who played football for Manchester United and Eire. He played in every position except goal, and he was one of the greatest captains the game has ever known. He smokes a pipe, speaks with a soft southern Irish accent and has a wonderful sense of humour that can even see the funny side of football. Anyone in the game will tell you, that takes some doing.

Carey had only been in the hospital a short time when he was racing Johnny Berry along the corridors. The little right-winger, who had played under Carey's captaincy for United, had just come round from his long five weeks' 'sleep'. He needed friends to talk football with him. Carey did that – and challenged him to a race. 'Johnny, you were always faster than me on a football field – let's see how fast you are now.' Johnny the joker did a lot for John Berry; and he had waited until the first hysteria of the crash had subsided before he came to see his old boss Matt Busby.

Said Carey: 'In the first few weeks you need the doctors and your family round your bedside. It's later on when you are getting better that you need your friends to rally round.'

Carey took time out from his long sessions with Matt Busby to come along and see me, to recount the story of how the Germans invited him to watch an operation. If it isn't true, it jolly well ought to be.

Carey with that rich Irish brogue told me: 'We were walking along the corridors, Mr Louis Edwards, the Manchester United director, Jimmy Murphy and myself. As usual I was smoking my pipe. We didn't notice where we were going till I looked up and saw a gang of fellows in white masks, and nurses in white masks too, clustered round an operating table. We turned to go back, but they were very sociable and waved us inside. When I was a youngster I fancied being a surgeon, so I stood just inside the door. The surgeon fellow looks up with the forceps in his hands and says very nice-like: "Good morning." So I said, as nice as I could: "Good morning." As I watched his nimble fingers he beckoned me to come right inside. As I didn't know what to do, I thought I'd better come nearer to the operating table. I got closer and closer until I was standing right beside them all. And I hadn't a sterile mask on either. Mind you, I was a gentleman – *I did knock my pipe out on the side of the operating table*.'

I nearly burst my chest plaster at that typically droll Carey joke. Most of all I liked it when he spoke of my Press colleagues: 'A terrible loss to the game of football, Frank. They were grand fellows and so experienced.'

And he got to reminiscing about them, and what a wonderful writer George Follows was. It was good to hear Carey talk that way, for I can remember the time George Follows, after reading an article written by Carey, remarked: 'It's a good job Johnny is going into football managership; if he turned to journalism we'd all be struggling to keep up with him.'

When he died George Follows was the top sports columnist of the *Daily Herald*. He had come a long way since I first met him in the Mulberry Tavern in Sheffield in 1948. At the time he was a straight newsman, first on the *Daily Mirror*, later on the *News Chronicle*. On every paper there is always a lot of argument. 'What sells the paper? News or Sport?'

I used to say: 'George, why don't you come on sport – where all the good writers are?'

Eventually George did. The man who had the brainwave was Mr Ralph McCarthy, then northern editor of the *News Chronicle*. The number of Ralph McCarthy's journalistic discoveries is legion. The switch of George Follows from news to sport was another winner. They sent Follows to a Yorkshire mining village and he began his story like this: 'The houses of M—— are back to back, simply because they dare not look one another in the face.'

He went to that horsy, expensive affair, the Doncaster yearling sales. His story began: 'The top price colt B—— at Doncaster yearling sales yesterday was 15,000 guineas. The top price in the horse-meat shop just down the road from the racecourse was 1/6 a pound. Seems even in the world of horses it all depends who your Dad was.'

When Bing Crosby came to England to play in the English Amateur Golf Championship the great names of Fleet Street excelled themselves in describing the Old Groaner Crosby crooning from bunker to bunker. Or claiming that Bing, humming 'When the Moon Comes Over the Mountains', was a little off-key with his golf at St Andrews.

Follows didn't take the obvious line on the story. He merely wrote: 'Harry L. Crosby (Virginia Springs, California) three-putted on the 18th green here at St Andrews tonight. St Andrews sighed. At last they could get back to golf.'

That was Follows, the miner's son from Staffordshire, who had the chance of taking up an academic career and picked the rough and tumble of journalism instead. An extraordinarily earthy yet literary man without inhibitions who was killed at forty, long before his time, just as he had put one foot on the pinnacle of his profession. A man with a thrilling turn of phrase which caused editors many times to send him messages of congratulation. A man who, had he lived, might so easily have become a short-story writer – an English Runyon, or a Paul Gallico.

That's why I was pleased to hear Johnny Carey remember George and Eric and Henry and Archie and the whole Press gang. For though football suffered grievous blows in the Munich crash, let no one doubt the losses to journalism were just as savage.

Then Johnny Carey switched from the sombre memories of the Press colleagues who had gone to more cheerful news. 'Looks as though Matt will be going home to England soon,' he said.

The more important question was still unanswered: Could Busby gather his physical strength; overcome the mental battle of losing so many of his friends – and still be a force in football?

19 The Courage of Matt Busby

Of all the many miracles of Munich, I think maybe the greatest of all was the way Matt Busby, Commander of the British Empire and now a knight, dragged himself up from the floor and came back to the game of football.

He was taken into Munich's Rechts der Isar Hospital with his life ebbing away, his life's work in ruins and many of his closest and dearest friends killed. The Germans, of course, did not know at first that he was a famous figure in British sport. To them he was just another patient, and a badly injured one at that. He could speak no word of German; his fame and contacts were of no use to him now. Only the *man* Busby mattered. Only his own physical strength and tremendous will power, allied to the skill of the doctors, could save him. He spoke the universal language all could understand by his flaming courage in adversity; his silent acceptance of the pain; his tremendous mental stamina when the full appalling details of the crash were revealed to him.

Think for a moment what the Munich Air Crash meant to Matt Busby.

If a painter spends a lifetime on a canvas and then has it destroyed by some malicious dauber, the world sympathises. Yet the painter can take up his brushes and create anew.

If a ballet dancer falls and sprains an ankle, the balletomanes howl their anguish at such bad luck. In time the dancer may yet come back quite as good as ever.

If an inventor wrecks his dream child, he still deals with materials; it is possible to try, try and try again.

In Busby's case his life work was founded on the skill of human beings. They were young men; they were his friends; they were as sons to him, as he watched them grow from boys into young men. He also lost close confidants like Walter

Crickmer, the United secretary; Bert Whalley, the United coach; Willie Satinoff; a close personal friend like Frank Swift, and the sports writers too.

I sometimes wonder whether people fully realise what all this meant to Busby, who was, so to speak, the centre-piece of it all.

Let me be quite brutally frank. Only a very remarkable man would have recovered from his injuries at Busby's age. Only a man with a sense of a mission yet unfulfilled would have come back to his job as Busby did.

When Busby lay desperately ill he was nearly drowned in the flood of letters, cables and telegrams from well-wishers all over the world. Yet, how quickly the public forget. When I got back to my sports desk in Manchester, I felt at times like puking. The snipers were after Busby; snipers more insidious in their way than the Germans who killed his father on the Somme. There were the anonymous letter-writers who fired in questions like these:

1. Why did Busby let that plane take off a third time, after two failures? He was in charge, he must have known something was wrong.

2. Just how badly was Busby hurt? Were all those stories just newspaper talk?

3. Why doesn't Busby get out? He'll never have the heart or the skill left to build a team like the old one he lost at Munich.

It's time someone spoke up for Busby on those points, and I'll do it for him.

Answer No. 1
Busby was not 100 per cent fit before the accident. He was not in charge of the travel arrangements or of the airworthiness of that aeroplane. Any one of us could have refused to fly. None of us did because we all – including Busby – thought the original trouble had been rectified after that second take-off.

Answer No. 2
How badly was Busby hurt? He sustained multiple injuries and severe shock after being catapulted out of the plane, by far the worst being the fact that his chest wall was crushed, thus endangering his lungs and his life.

Answer No. 3

The 'knockers' who said Busby was finished forgot they said exactly the same in 1953 when his team slumped and he started to build the side that became known as the Busby Babes. When he returned to work after the crash he quickly paid the British record fee of £45,000 to Sheffield Wednesday for Albert Quixall; and £30,000 for Maurice Setters, the Under-23 international. There is not much sentiment in the high-pressure business of soccer managership; but, as always, he went for the class performer, to try and bring back to his team some of their glamour and former greatness.

You cannot lose a complete half-back line of the calibre of Eddie Colman, Mark Jones and Duncan Edwards – plus of course Jackie Blanchflower – without feeling the impact. That half-back line was perhaps the greatest club half-back line ever marshalled by one team in Britain. Yes, I know the old-timers will fume and talk about Duckworth, Roberts and Bell; about the pre-First World War Manchester United; of Sunderland, and of Rangers – Colman, Jones (or Blanchflower) and Edwards took on the best teams in Europe and still looked great, in this high-class company.

Roger Byrne had plenty of critics, but England found him hard to replace at left-back. Great footballers like Joe Mercer, then Aston Villa's manager, will tell you that Byrne was great; fit to be mentioned in the same breath as such immortal full-backs as Warney Cresswell, Ernie Blenkinsop, Johnny Carey, Tom Cooper and Roy Goodall.

Tommy Taylor, as a centre-forward, often took a beating from the critics. Even my good friend Henry Rose once wrote of him: 'If Tommy Taylor is the best centre-forward in England, I am Santa Claus.' But Big Tommy from Barnsley, the lad with the ever-ready smile and all-action power-play as an attack leader, was sorely missed. Tommy may not have been a Tommy Lawton or a Dixie Dean or a Hughie Gallacher, but on his day he was the best in the business, a header in the Lawton-Lofthouse class, and, as Roger Byrne once remarked to me: 'Tommy's greatest asset – and sometimes his greatest fault – is that he gets in such wonderful positions, always looking for the ball, always taking a pounding in the middle and taking the weight off the other forwards. If he had Hughie Gallacher's ball control he would be the greatest ever – but then, Hughie probably wasn't as good in the air as Tom.'

Can you imagine how Matt Busby felt when he first heard these wonderful friends of his had gone? For three weeks after Duncan Edwards died the conspiracy of silence which kept the news from Busby was safely preserved, until a priest inadvertently let it slip out. Only those close to the Manchester United manager know what a desperate struggle the doctors had with him in the days that followed that revelation.

I still marvel how Matt Busby, in a matter of weeks, pulled himself back from the Vale of Shadows to become recognisable as the man football had known so well. I still see Busby, in the mind's eye, after the doctors had told him he could leave Munich and come back to see his team play in the Cup Final at Wembley against Bolton Wanderers.

Thursday, April 18th, 1958, is a day I won't forget, as Busby, pale and very shaky on his legs, eased his way through the door of Room 401. He could just manage about ten yards without sitting down, but he made an effort at that jaunty walk. The old familiar greeting: 'Hello, my old pal, hope you won't be long following Jean and me back to England. I'll bet you're longing to see those two boys of yours.'

In ten weeks Busby had made a staggering recovery from the shell of a man they found on Munich Airport. As he came across the floor of my room a twinge of pain crossed that craggy face. 'I'm afraid they won't have me in the First Team yet, Frank lad,' he managed to smile.

Of the crash he said little, except that he had felt a sudden veering to the right and that he had put up his hand as one might in a car to protect his face from a splintering windscreen. Then oblivion, until, like me, he awoke in hospital.

For a moment I feared he might break down, as he spoke of Bert Whalley, always so fit and full of vitality, killed in the seat next to him.

Busby then gave a fleeting clue to the long hours of agony he had suffered. 'So many times I have asked myself,' he told me, 'whether there was anything I could do, or ought to have done, to stop that plane. But you saw how it was. We went back to the terminal building, and everything seemed to have been checked.

It would have been as pointless for me to ask the pilot if everything was OK as if he had asked me whether I had picked the best team for Manchester United! All you can do is repose confidence in the pilots and airline. After all, no pilot would take a chance, for his life is just as much at stake as yours.'

I agreed with Busby then, just as I do now. It is easy, and painful after the accident, to say we should not have gone; but at the time there seemed no apparent reason why we shouldn't try to take off for England.

I felt terribly lonely as Busby slipped out of the door and I waved my hand to his wife Jean. 'See you in Chorlton-cum-Hardy when we get back to Manchester.' The television cameras whirred, and the posse of Pressmen dashed away with the Busby party. In the hospital's big hallway, he said his goodbyes to Professors Maurer, Kessel and all the other doctors and nurses who had looked after him so well. Then Matt and his wife boarded the Rheingold Express for an overland journey back home, with Des Hackett of the *Daily Express* and his colleague, cameraman Bill Gregory, to keep them company. I was left alone with my wife, the last of the Munich survivors. I didn't know it then, but I was to stay in Munich another eleven weeks.

Somehow the place didn't seem to be so dull when a cable arrived the next day from the Hook of Holland from Matt, Jean, Des Hackett and Bill Gregory. It read briefly: '*Get stripped son. You're on next.*'

That's how Busby left Munich to take up his job at Old Trafford and to go to Wembley to see Manchester United well beaten in the Cup Final 2–0 by Bolton Wanderers.

In his first full season back at the helm, Manchester United, after a shocking start to the season, hit a phenomenal streak and finished runners-up to Wolves. No one was more surprised than Matt Busby. He told me at the time: 'All I was hoping for was a reasonably safe place in the First Division until we get things sorted out. These boys have played better than I dared hope. But a lot has to be done. It will take years to try and build up again.'

That was just what Matt Busby, with Jimmy Murphy still at his side, set out to do. Was he right or wrong, to try and build a great football team again after all the fearful heartbreak and the great human tragedy of Munich?

I am quite sure he was right. Busby's family and close friends know that his health almost cracked under the strain, trying to get back into top gear too soon after Munich. He had to give up his job as Scotland's team manager and was advised to take a prolonged rest from his duties with Manchester United. Why didn't he? Say what you like about Busby, but he has never been a quitter. Only sometimes the shadows crossed that face as he whispered hoarsely to his closest friends: '*Sometimes I STILL SEE THEM PLAY.*'

20 Why Did We Crash?

When Matt Busby left Munich I was the solitary survivor left behind, 1,000 miles from home, wondering deep in my heart whether things would be different now that the most famous figure among us had departed. The tragedy came clearer into focus; especially one day when I had a welcome visitor, Captain James Thain, the commander of our plane. I admired the man for coming in to see one of his passengers in such circumstances. One glance at his face showed that though he had escaped serious physical injury, he had suffered deep mental stresses and he was even then under the heavy burden of facing the official German enquiry into the crash.

What was the mystery behind that crash? Why should such a safe aeroplane as an Elizabethan roar down a runway, hurtling on and on and never rise into the air? When death and disaster strike at high speed, even those in control must find it hard to get every incident into coherent form. As one of the survivors, I have found it most interesting to read and digest the torrent of words and theories which have been spilled about this accident. Would it be out of place now to put forward my opinions?

For years after the Munich Air Crash the armchair critics were seeking to establish why this accident happened. Questions were asked in Parliament; the air correspondents, perhaps prompted by interested parties, thrashed out thousands of words, giving their verdict.

I don't suppose anyone will ever pin-point the exact cause of such a tragedy. In all accidents such as this, one is left with the unhappy conclusion that a combination of factors piled up one upon the other. If at any stage this sequence of events had been broken, then the accident could have been averted or, one thinks, the death-roll would not have been so high.

For instance, having plunged through the perimeter fence, if the house had not been there and if the wing had not been torn off as it struck the house, surely it would have been possible to pull up with perhaps nothing worse than a severe shaking up, and a few bruises for the passengers?

But the house was there. You may argue it was an unnecessary hazard so close to an airfield. The answer to that is that one doesn't expect aeroplanes to overrun the perimeter fence anyway. They are supposed to fly over the perimeter fences of airfields.

Another question repeatedly fired at me has been: 'Why on earth did you get aboard that aeroplane after it had failed twice to take off? If you were in a motor car and it broke down, you would never dream of driving away in it until the fault had been rectified.'

How easy to say that *now*. There were forty-four people in that airliner; anyone could have said: 'I'm not going up in that thing!'

No one did. Why? Because the plane went back to the terminal buildings where the ground crew and the pilots discussed the failures. As passengers we assumed they had solved the fault. The engines were run up before the crash, and found OK. They have been tested since, and the air experts have ruled out engine failure as a possible cause of the accident.

We now come to the next question: Why was it the commander of the airliner, Captain Thain, sat in the right-hand seat monitoring the instruments, while the second pilot, Captain Rayment, made the three take-off attempts, handling the controls? Why in fact didn't the skipper of the plane take complete control?

Anyone making a close study of the enquiry report will find that Captain Thain flew the machine out from Manchester to Belgrade, with Captain Rayment flying it on the return trip. Captain Rayment had in fact over 3,000 flying hours on Elizabethans, which was nearly twice as many as Captain Thain. They both held equal rank. Both were experienced pilots.

I was told that when Manchester United chartered the plane, Captain Thain was given the command of this flight and Captain Rayment, who was just coming back to duty after a spell in hospital, was given duties as co-pilot. With his vast experience, there seemed no logical reason why he should not be at the controls on take-off. With a less-experienced man as co-pilot, one is left wondering whether Captain Thain would not have made the take-off attempts himself, although whether this would have averted the accident must be in grave doubt. It might however explain the suggestion of divided responsibility in the cockpit.

Captain Thain told the German enquiry that he banged the throttles for more power and tried to retract the undercarriage, while there is some evidence that Captain Rayment was trying to slow the machine up by applying the brakes. At that tremendous ground speed, with an accident looming ahead, men react differently in emergency, and no man can really recall the whole sequence of events or of his reactions. In any case, these things are for the aerodynamic experts. To the lay mind, there is one question that overrides all:

Why didn't the aeroplane lift from the ground and fly away before it was anywhere near the end of the runway or the perimeter fence?

The runway at Munich is 1,908 metres long, and we travelled a further distance of 450 metres before the front part of the plane skidded to rest – in all a distance of 2,358 metres, well over a mile, without ever getting into the air. Quite obviously there was something radically wrong.

The arguments about the cause of the disaster appear to be narrowed down to these two:

1. Formation of ice on the wings, or
2. Slush on the runway causing the aircraft to brake just as flying speed was reached.

The German enquiry decided that formation of ice on the wings was the major cause of the crash.

The main factors to back up that decision were that sixteen aircraft landed and took off safely from Munich that afternoon. All were de-iced; none reported any impediment on take-off worthy of mention. The Germans had a car on the runway with an expert checking the depth of slush even as our aircraft was trying to take off. They claimed that, even if slush had packed the wheels and the brakes, the airliner should have taken off after rolling 1,080 metres down the runway, whereas if there were 5 mm of ice on the wings – this was later established – the aeroplane could not have risen into the air within take-off distance of 2,270 metres. That is, of course, beyond the perimeter fence.

The one flaw in the German technical argument was that *the wings were not checked until six hours after the crash*, following a further heavy fall of snow. By that time they found a layer of ice under powdery snow, about 5 mm thick.

The plain truth is that all the technical arguments in the world do not bring back those who lost their lives.

And to my mind there was at times too much of the national prestige angle in the arguments that raged after the crash, in questions asked by the MPs, and in the statements by people who had an axe to grind! I make one humble plea. Cut out of the mind all the hysteria, the crocodile tears, the snap judgements. Take the trouble to read the official German enquiry.

1. What were the de-icing safeguards for the Elizabethans?

2. Was the Elizabethan de-iced, and if not, why not?

3. As all other companies de-iced their aircraft, are we to assume they merely did so to find their ground crews work for the day, and that there was really no necessity to do so?

4. If slush caused the plane to slow up on the third run, why was this hazard not noticed before?

5. After the two failures, were the wheels and brakes examined for any packing of snow and ice?

6. Were the runways swept after the crash to make sure the aeroplanes which took off later were not hindered?

7. The Germans claimed they had an expert on the runway checking for slush. Did this gentlemen at any time stop other aircraft from taking off on account of slush?

8. When an aircraft fails to take off in its normal take-off area, what are the emergency stop methods used by the crew? Do they brake? Retract the undercarriage and shut the engines off? Or do they push ahead with full power to try and get the plane off the ground?

9. In the war-time RAF it was always the rigger's responsibility to make sure the plane was de-iced before it took off. No rigger or airframe fitter would ever sign for it as being airworthy, no matter how high the rank of the pilot, and no matter what he would say. In BEA, is this the ground crew's responsibility, or does it rest with the air crew? Or is it a matter of consultation between both parties?

10. The Germans claimed every other plane was de-iced that day. If this was so, were the pilots of our plane told of this safety measure by the other airline companies?

Those are the questions – I wonder whether anyone will ever find the answers.

21 The Prayers Have Been Answered

Take it from me, it is not funny lying week after week cooped up in plaster like a gruesome marionette. It becomes bearable, I found, in the happy company of your fellow patients; and by reading of great and arduous deeds like Hillary's ascent of Everest; Sir Winston Churchill's *History of the Second World War*; or *The Kon-Tiki Expedition.* I had some good friends in the publishing world in England – like Bill Luscombe of Stanley Paul – who kept me plentifully supplied with books. The world of words is an escape for those who are bedridden. When you read, for instance, of Sir Edmund Hillary and Sherpa Tensing perched up there in the icy blasts on the face of Everest – why, a mere plaster confining the movements of the body seems nothing at all! My fellow patients, now that my English friends had departed, were of course Germans. They laughed and joked and kept up the high spirits just as one sees in English hospitals. Like Richard Leppla, a blond, square-jawed man, who arrived one day in some agony. He had a great pile of flying books by his bedside, and I was somewhat surprised at one of his first questions: 'Have you met this man Group Captain Bader? I have read with great interest his book. A great pilot; what a man he must be.'

Leppla admitted, in an offhand sort of way, he had been in the German Air Force himself during the last war. Not until some time later did I discover he had been a fighter-pilot himself on the Polish Front, then in France, over Britain and on the Eastern Front until he had lost his left eye in an aerial battle. There are those who carry the wounds of war far into the days of peace; and probably such people could not have made friends with Dick Leppla at any price. I can only record that although he was a patient he acted more like a nurse to me – making sure we had the windows open; the telephone near at hand; and that I had everything I required within easy reach. Every night before he fell asleep he would say: 'If you need anything, Frank, I am here. If you have pains you must let me know and I will call the nurses for you. We get you fit soon, I hope.'

Leppla's sense of humour was as infectious as his kindness. I was saying to him one day: 'When I was in Sidi Barrani, old boy.' He was anxious to hear all about the famous catch-phrase of Kenneth Horne and Dickie Murdoch. I explained it to him. Next day Leppla walked in backwards, his cap on back to front, and saluted the back of his head very solemnly, intoning: '*Ven I vos in Smolensk, Herr Taylor.*'

I asked him once what he thought about the English countryside and he grinned mischievously. 'Frank, please. Your RAF is very good and I am going too fast in the war to notice such things.'

Not until he left the hospital did I find out that he had escaped six times from his Russian captors; that despite the loss of his eye over Leningrad he managed to get back into the German Air Force and reach a high-ranking position. When I asked him why he should want to go back into flying after surviving the war he replied simply: 'It is my life.' Although they were enemies once, I think it is a point of view that Group Captain Bader and his fellow air aces of the RAF would have understood.

On the Queen's Birthday Mr J. Somers-Cocks, the British Consul in Munich, who with his wife had gone far beyond the bounds of duty in looking after the needs of the injured and their womenfolk, arrived with a large bottle of champagne. It was one of the most moving moments in my life when the British Consul, the ex-German fighter-pilot Lt.-Col. Leppla, Doktor (of Engineering) Johannes Gieth of the German Patent Office, my wife and I toasted the Queen – in a German hospital.

This same Dr Gieth translated one of the funniest stories I've ever heard concerning Hitler. At one time Sister Gilda, who nursed us so well, had had Eva Braun, Hitler's mistress, as a patient. When the Nazi hierarchy arrived there was much heel-clicking and 'Heiling' with the right arms outstretched, but the little nun Sister Gilda had conveniently taken hold of a *Schüssel* (bed-pan) of Eva Braun's. To salute Nazi fashion would have emptied the contents all over the Fuehrer! To see the small nun with the little-girl expression on her face trying to explain her dilemma half in English and half in German was really a riot.

There is not much room for nationalistic feeling in a hospital where close and intimate comradeship among the sick means so much. It is impossible perhaps to translate into words all the innumerable little acts of kindness which broke down the narrow barriers of nationalism.

There were many English visitors, too, passing through Munich on their holidays, who came to the hospital. Aston Villa, with their manager Eric Houghton, directors and other officials, came to see me five times in three days. What a wonderful tonic that was, to have chaps like Peter McParland, Nigel Sims, Jackie Sewell, Jimmy Dugdale, Stan Lynn and the rest of the Villa players clustered round the bed passing on all the latest news of football in England!

There is a wonderful comradeship in sport – even if sometimes football clubs and football players may violently disagree with what we sports writers say about the game. There is comradeship in the Press as well. Not a week passed without some of the Munich journalists – whom I'd never even met before the accident – coming in to talk about newspapers and their problems in German journalism. And they always saw to it that there was a plentiful supply of Munich beer!

Eve Boswell, famed TV singer who was appearing in Munich, sent in a huge bunch of flowers and a 'get well soon' message – a mostly kindly gesture.

The days rolled on endlessly. April into May, then June. As June drew to a close, I had yet another visitor from England: Dr Frank Preston of BEA. 'Professor Maurer says you are now fit to travel home if you like,' he said. 'There is nothing more they can do for you here. We must wait and see whether any further surgery is needed, and if it is, it won't be for several weeks.'

Going home after twenty-one weeks – it was unbelievable. Home to my sons Andrew and Alastair – I couldn't play cricket with them or even walk yet, but at least, after the weeks of doubt and worry, I would be seeing them again.

Fräulein Ilse Reuss from the physiotherapy department, who had worked hard to get Matt Busby walking and who had for weeks and weeks meticulously been massaging my fingers, left arm and shoulder to get them moving again, now came in with crutches. While she stood on one side, Sister Gilda on the other and Professor Kessel at my back in case I fell, we made some hilarious progress across the room and into the corridor. The right leg swung helplessly in plaster; the left felt like rubber – but I was moving after a fashion. In this way it would be possible to go back by train, ambulance and ship to England.

July 2nd, 1958, was Homegoing Day – the day of many goodbyes: to Leppla, to Dr Gieth, to Dr Oppelt, Dr Gross, Father Angelo. They were so many.

Professor Kessel bounced swiftly across the room. 'You've made it, Frank. Good luck. I hope to see you at the Cup Final – with our team, Manchester United, of course!'

Then it was Professor Maurer, with a melon-sized smile, holding out those thick, but so skilful fingers to shake hands. I asked him to have a farewell drink, although it was still only morning. He shook his head and touched his heart. 'I would like to do so, but this would not be good for my patients, when I start to operate in a few minutes.'

How could I thank this man? I began: 'What can I say, Professor? I was in the war five and a half years; now I owe my left arm, my right leg and my life to the skill of German doctors and nurses.'

He smiled understandingly. 'We did nothing, Herr Taylor. For three days the Angels looked after you – then we did our best. Medicine is international, we have been glad to do what we could for all of you.' He gripped me with both hands, chuckled as he had done so many times before; then that stocky, electric figure was gone.

Sister Solemnis, who had kept constant vigil by my bedside in the early weeks after the accident, came in at night to say goodbye. She was so young and so dedicated to her calling and by this time she had been transferred to another part of the hospital to nurse some people very badly injured in a tram smash. 'I hope you soon have your good health back,' she said. 'I prayed for you many times. I think the prayers have been answered.'

'Thank you for all you have done for me,' I replied. It was all I could think of at the time.

We were leaving on the midnight train: my wife; George Vine, the *News Chronicle* correspondent in Germany; Herr Roger Rother, BEA airport superintendent at Munich; a nursing Sister of BEA, and myself.

At eleven o'clock at night I was wheeled out of Room 401 on the fourth floor. At the head of the stairs Sister Gilda was waiting. She had stayed up long past her bedtime to say goodbye to the last of the survivors. This tiny woman, with the warm, frank eyes, who had smoothed Matt Busby's brow in his direst hour; who had treated us all as though we were her children. I wanted to throw my hands round her neck and kiss her – but the thought was repressed. One doesn't kiss a nun. Then how does one say goodbye to such a woman, who had dedicated her life to God and the self-effacing profession of nursing? I took her hands in mine and gripped them tight. 'You, Sister Gilda, have been a second mother to me, to Matt Busby, Jack Blanchflower, Johnny Berry and all the rest of us. We can never forget your kindness.'

She gripped my hands and murmured half in German, half in English: 'Good night. . .*Auf Wiedersehen*. . . pleasant journey. Come back to see us. God bless you.'

I turned to see that soft, motherly figure in her vast white cap at the head of the stairs, as she waved her hand. Then we were gone, down the four floors and outside into the ambulance. Through the night it sped, past the neon signs and the well-lighted shops. The sudden rush of the vehicle after the months of inaction produced an uncontrollable trembling. It was as though we were speeding down the runway again. My wife gripped my arm as I lay tense on the stretcher.

'It's all right,' she said, 'look at the shops – the hotel where Mrs Busby and all of us stayed.'

I looked out into the night. So this was Munich, the city I had never seen except from the air. Munich, the End of the Road for Bert Whalley, Walter Crickmer, Tom Curry, Willie Satinoff, Tom Cable, Bela Miklos, eight young Manchester United footballers and eight of my Press colleagues.

'So long, Munich,' I whispered to myself as we sped to the railway station. 'One day I will come back on my own two legs.'

22   How I Recovered

The greatest thrill of my life was when, in 1960, I walked through the main doors of the Rechts der Isar Hospital in Ismaninger Strasse, Munich. I felt like a man re-born – as no doubt I am.

I have in fact been back to Munich many times – including the 1972 Olympic Games – when the staff of the Rechts der Isar were instrumental in saving the life of a colleague, Jim Manning, after he had suffered a heart attack.

A great deal has happened in the 25 years since the Munich Disaster.

Captain Thain, the commander of our ill-fated aircraft, died after a long and bitter struggle to clear his name. With the help of his wife, a science teacher, he was able to prove that slush on the runway played a significant part in our failure to take off, and that discovery has no doubt saved the lives of many many air passengers since then.

Professor Frank Kessel, the neurosurgeon who became such a close friend, died in 1974.

In 1980, as I was preparing to fly to Moscow for the Olympic Games, I had a message from friends in Munich that Professor Maurer, the man who played the biggest role in saving so many lives, had died in retirement, after a coronary attack. I immediately wrote to Matt Busby, to alert him to this sad news, only to get the worrying information that Matt himself had had a coronary attack. Happily he has recovered.

Ted Ellyard, one of the heroes of the crash, became a colleague when we both worked on the *Daily Herald* in Manchester. Alas, after I moved to London I was saddened to learn that he had died from a coronary.

As for the players, *Bobby Charlton* is now a world wide figure in soccer, honoured by Her Majesty the Queen with the CBE for his services to Football. Today Bobby is a director of Wigan Athletic, a businessman and a part-time commentator with BBC TV.

Bill Foulkes and *Dennis Viollet* are working with soccer clubs in the United States.

Harry Gregg, former manager of Shrewsbury, was also a coach for Manchester United until 1981.

Ray Wood I met in the Arab Emirates, where he had been a soccer coach after a coaching assignment in Kenya.

And my Yugoslav friend Nebosja Tomasevich is a famous editor, and author.

As for me . . . well let me take you back to the time when I left Munich, in June 1958, still unable to walk . . .

I lay on a stretcher aboard the Rheingold Express, as it thundered northwards along the west bank of the Rhine, looking out over that famous river – once described by Churchill as Germany's Lifeline – and reflected on the strange twists of fortune which had brought me into this present situation.

Six months previously, there had seemed scarcely a cloud on the horizon. I had a happy marriage, and two small sons with whom I loved to play soccer and cricket. I had a good job as Chief Northern Sports Writer on the *News Chronicle*. I was already the 'ghost' author of six books in collaboration with famous sports personalities and I was rapidly building up a solid association with Eddie Waring, who was just starting his television career with a sports programme from Manchester.

Now, what would the future hold for me?

All my closest friends on newspapers had been killed, and that made me feel very sad and lonely. I was determined to see their relatives and loved ones to tell them they had not suffered, and yet I wondered how they would feel, meeting me, the sole survivor among the sports writers. I felt guilty about being the only one to have lived through that tragedy.

I looked down at my shattered right leg still in plaster, and wondered how much longer I would have to lie like this, either flat on my back in bed, or else wheeled along in a wheelchair with my leg propped up. At the back of my mind was the ever-present fear that the surgeons might still have to amputate.

I looked at my wife Peggy, and thought of my two sons Andrew and Alastair. I was coming home to see them for the first time for almost six months. and that thought cleared my mind of all depression. I was alive, and while there was life there was hope. It was true I could only just move the fingers of my left hand, and I couldn't even raise my left arm above my head . . . but I would do it, I swore I would do it. If I didn't have faith, there was no way the surgeons, however skilled they were, could get me back on my feet and working.

Perhaps it was as well that I didn't realise, on that journey home, just how long it was going to take before the orthopaedic surgeons finished their work.

I had been transferred from the Rechts der Isar Hospital in Munich to the London Clinic, in the care of Mr Derek Coltart. He performed a pinch graft, removing small circles of flesh from my backside and transplanting them on to my shin to seal off the wounds. There were several other operations in the eight months I was under his care.

Just before Christmas, 1958, he sent me home, with crutches and a walking plaster. 'Come back and see me in a month to see if it has worked,' he said cheerfully.

On the morning I went back to his surgery, I was only a few yards from his door, when I felt something go. I couldn't advance another yard, so I just stood, with my weight on my left leg, my crutches propped against the wall, until they could get a stretcher.

When Coltart saw me he shook his head. 'I am sorry,' he said. 'It was only a fibrous union. The bones have not joined together.' He wanted to continue treating me at the Clinic, but I felt I couldn't spend any more time in London and decided that it was time to go home to Manchester.

From Matt Busby there came the message:

'Stick to it, son. You'll make it.' He knew, even if I didn't, that there was still a long way to go. Happily my case was transferred to Park Hospital, Davyhulme, where I came under the care of Matron McManus, Sister Goldstraw, and, most important of all, John (later Sir John) Charnley, one of the finest orthopaedic surgeons in the world.

His first words struck a chill of fear in my heart:

'Very interesting, but a nasty one,' he said. 'You realise, if we amputate, you can be walking on an artificial limb in perhaps three months.'

His manner was brisk and forthright and he must have seen my face fall when he mentioned amputation. I realise now, he was probably testing my reaction. If this was so, he soon found out how I felt.

'Amputate?' I cried. 'Surely to God they would have done that right at the start had it been necessary. What would you do if it was your leg?' I added in a panic.

This shy, somewhat self-effacing world-renowned surgeon, looked me in the eye. 'How long have we got?' he asked. 'You must realise we are virtually starting again from scratch, a year after the accident. I can try a bone graft and clean up the whole area, although the graft may be rejected first time, and then we would have to do it all over again. You must prepare yourself to spend another year in hospital . . .' he broke off to smile. 'But I sincerely hope we can make it sooner than that.'

As his patient, I found that Charnley – as with Maurer, Kessel and Lechner – had this remarkable gift of giving those they cared for every confidence in their skill. And so it proved for me.

On Monday, August 24th, 1959 – 18 months and three weeks after I had been hauled out of that wrecked Elizabethan airliner – I lay on an X-ray table at Park Hospital, Davyhulme, as Mr Charnley examined, first my leg and then the X-ray plates he held in his hand. I scarcely dared breathe. All those months I had lain helpless, wondering fearfully whether every knock on the door would announce that the surgeons had failed, and that my right leg would, after all, have to come off. Yes, for more than 18 months, I had lived with that terrible nagging fear. Now, this was the moment of truth. I looked at Charnley closely to see if there were any signs of success.

'All right,' he said briskly, 'don't be afraid. Hop down.'

I was petrified in case that leg would buckle under me yet again. With the assistance of his physiotherapist Miss Robinson and the radiographer, I gingerly lowered my feet to the floor. They felt firm enough, so I tried to walk, putting one foot in front of the other very carefully. I tried to move a little faster, and, like a baby walking for the first time, had very little sense of balance. I tottered a few more yards before I stopped. This was absolutely marvellous.

I wasn't too sure of myself, but at least I could move under my own steam. I was no longer dependent on others to take me from one place to another. Yes, thanks to God, I could walk again, for the first time since I had walked out with Frank Swift across the tarmac at Munich to board the Elizabethan airliner.

I turned to thank Charnley, but he had already gone to attend another patient in his over-crowded clinic. He had finished this case, now there were others more in need of his skilful surgery. That's the way it is for surgeons like Charnley. They work, along with their nurses and physiotherapists, attending the sick and the maimed, far from the public eye, with naught to sustain them but the call of mercy; the sense of dedication to a noble profession; and the thanks of their grateful patients.

I personally can never repay the debts I owed to men like Maurer, Kessel, Lechner, Coltart and Charnley. Because of them I can walk, and was made well again, and although at first I still needed sticks and crutches, I was able to take up my duties full time on the *News Chronicle*, just in time for the re-start of the 1959–60 Soccer season.

The next obstacle for me was simply this: would I have the guts to fly again?

When I was leaving the Munich Hospital Professor Maurer at first wanted me to fly home, and I was not the least worried. He said he thought I had the right temperament, but in fact the plan fell through. When I did fly again, it was May, 1960, and I was due to travel with England's Under-23 team to East Berlin, Warsaw, Istanbul and Tel Aviv. The man in charge of the team was a young manager at the start of his career – a man called Ron Greenwood.

By this time, I had had two years of desperate struggle to get back on my feet. It was vital for me to accept this challenge in order to take up my career again, flying anywhere in the world at the behest of my office and newspaper. I do not deny that I wondered, at times, whether it would be worth the effort. Could I really expect that a man like me, with only 50 per cent movement in my left arm, a right leg three inches shorter than the left, plus a rigid right ankle, would be able to compete again in the rough and tumble of daily journalism? I wasn't badly handicapped, but I didn't want any favours either. When two newspapermen are racing for the one and only telephone, there is no time for the ordinary courtesies of life. Apart from that, since I had got rid of all my plasters I had developed feelings of claustrophobia. I no longer travelled by underground because I felt trapped. Nor did I like travelling alone in a lift in case it jammed between floors. I still do not know why I had this feeling, when all the time I was in hospital I never felt the slightest fear in a lift, whether I was in a hospital bed or invalid chair. Now I was undeniably panicky in enclosed spaces.

As the day of my first aeroplane trip came nearer, I started to worry even more and blurted out these fears to my doctor in Manchester.

He laughed and shook his head. 'I think you are worrying unnecessarily. In my opinion you are the phlegmatic type who won't turn a hair.'

'It is all very well you saying that,' I replied, 'when we are safe on the ground. But I don't know how I will feel when they shut the door of the cabin and the engines rev up. I might lose my head completely and make a dash for the door.'

'If you feel like that I'll give you a pill to keep you quiet on the first trip, but I'll take a bet that you won't need another pill on your second flight.'

He was right. I very carefully took a pill two hours before take-off, and then another just before we were ready to go. I carefully strapped myself in, took out my dental plate and looked out of the window as our aircraft waited at the end of the runway at Heathrow.

I was sitting with an old friend, Jack Wood of the *Daily Mail*, who had himself been lucky enough to survive when his bomber crashed in the war. As we started to roll, he kept up an incessant chatter telling jokes as I sat silently looking at my watch. I wanted to be sure we were off the ground before 40 seconds had elapsed, otherwise I thought we might overshoot the runway as we had done at Munich.

As the engines reached their maximum thrust I felt a surge of confidence. I could feel the wheels leave the ground and hear them snap into position as they were retracted. I had a soaring feeling of euphoria, the kind of feeling you get when you hear

you have passed a particularly difficult examination, on which
your whole future rests.

'Beaten the B——,' I said under my breath. Jack Wood was
still chattering away, doing his best to keep my mind off the
take-off. 'You can shut up, Jack,' I said, 'I could fly this bloody
thing myself now.'

I was of course just being cocky. Strange to say, I have never
completely lost that feeling, even though I have flown
thousands of miles since then. The routine is always the same. I
fasten my seat belt firmly, sitting as relaxed as I can, listening to
the cabin crew going through the routine safety precautions.
Once we start rolling I check my watch and note the number of
seconds it takes to get airborne. I now have a fairly good idea just
how long it takes for a 737, a 707, a Jumbo and a DC 10 to get
airborne.

I knew that many of my colleagues and some of the young
players were eyeing me curiously on that first flight, wondering
whether I would be jumpy, or whether my nerve would crack. It
is not a question of courage or even of stupid bravado.
Whenever I feel any qualms, or have any doubts and nagging
fears on a long haul, I automatically recall the words of my very
good friend, Professor Frank Kessel.

'The lights went out for you, and you awoke in our hospital.
The lights went out for your friends and they have awakened in
eternity. It is anybody's guess which is the best place to be,' he
once told me.

There was an even more extraordinary experience a year later,
when once again I was detailed to travel with the England
Under-23 team on their tour to Yugoslavia, Romania and Israel.
This time Joe Mercer, the former England, Everton and Arsenal
captain, was manager of the squad. We touched down at
Munich to refuel, and as we were about to take off, on the same
runway on which the Manchester United charter aircraft had
crashed, a violent electric storm broke overhead. The reassuring
voice of the captain, explained why we had stopped on the
runway. I was sitting next to Joe Mercer. I looked at him. He
looked at me, and winked!

I must confess my first thought was to ask the cabin crew to
open the doors so that I could get out. I reasoned that, if only
someone had done that on our ill fated take-off in 1958, no one

would have been killed. No sooner had that thought crystallised in my mind, than I dismissed it, because I realised every eye of the England party was upon me, wondering how I would react. If I got out of my seat no doubt everyone else would do the same. Besides, supposing I asked to leave the aircraft, what would happen to my luggage? and how would I get to Belgrade to report the match for the *News Chronicle*?

So I looked at Joe Mercer and smiled back at him, and, like the rest of the party, sat patiently until we took off.

Those two England tours gave me the confidence I needed to carry on my profession as a sports writer. Nevertheless, when I came back to the soccer circuit, I found something was missing. Perhaps it was the loss of my fellow sports writers, but I began to feel that I ought to widen my horizons and not become type-cast as a soccer reporter and nothing else.

Apart from that, my return to work coincided with the celebrated George Eastham case, when the famous Newcastle United, Arsenal and England player won a High Court Action against the restrictions imposed on the earnings of professional footballers employed by Football League Clubs.

When professionalism was introduced into English football, the League clubs decided they would not pay extra wages to star players. They wanted everybody to be equal, and therefore the contract, which all professional players signed, not only tied them to their clubs, but also stipulated the maximum and minimum wages the players were entitled to get.

Eastham and his legal advisers claimed that a player was entitled to negotiate his own contract and be paid what he thought his talents were worth. It was a Court battle to free the players from what their former Union Chairman Jimmy Guthrie had described as 'Soccer slavery.'

Once Eastham had won his case, the style of English soccer was changed. It opened the door to the first £100 a week footballer, Johnny Haynes, whereas prior to the Eastham case, the maximum wage for players of the calibre of Bobby Charlton was pegged at £20 a week.

I was only one of many sports writers who had repeatedly urged in newspaper articles that players must be allowed to cash in on their talents because their careers were so short. Nevertheless, after being out of action for so long undergoing hospital treatment, the soccer matches I was now watching and reporting bore little resemblance to the aggressive open style I had been used to. With incentive bonuses and crowd attendance bonuses, losing matches could now cost players a lot of money. Thus was born what became known as possession football, where the side which had the ball passed it across the field, or back to the goalkeeper, in any type of manoeuvre to prevent the other side getting possession. Players like Raich Carter, Don Revie and Johnny Haynes, stylish players who excited the crowds with their long accurate passes in an open-style of play, now became redundant.

The Eastham Case, in my opinion, not only caused a revolution in the pay structure of footballers, it also brought about a revolution in the traditional England game, of a midfield general and fast raiding wingers.

Perhaps the last great exponents of this traditional English style, in the Football League, were Tottenham Hotspur in 1961 when they became the first club this century to do the double (ie. win the League Championship and the FA Cup in the same season).

As British footballers tried to master the delicate ball control and the techniques of the Latin-Americans, so too, did the English style of robust tackling disappear. As a neutral soccer reporter, I found that when there was hard, vigorous and robust play on the field, I never had to report crowd disturbances. As the English game changed its style, the charging of goalkeepers became a thing of the past and much of the former robust play disappeared from our game, which now attracted the kind of spectator who seemed more concerned with starting a fight on the terraces than watching the play.

No doubt Freud could explain why, as British football became daintier, more tactically aware, and imported some of the continental and Latin-American style, it attracted a more violent type of spectator! As a reporter I found I spent more time reporting crowd disturbances, and recording the quotes and views of managers on the way their team played, than in actually giving an old-fashioned neutral opinion. I know what my friends Henry Rose, George Follows and Eric Thompson would have thought of this new reporting style, so I decided to widen my experience by becoming more involved in other sports.

But for this, a happy decision, I would not have enjoyed the challenge and the variety of reporting so many other sports. The Tokyo, Mexico, Munich, Montreal and Moscow Olympic Games are now among my scrapbook of sporting memories.

I was very lucky to survive the Munich Air Crash. And I have been lucky to travel so far and wide since then, even to China, and as far as Tashkent and Samarkand in the Soviet Union.

Yet always at the back of my mind, I carry the memories of Munich and of the great Manchester United team, and of the marvellous colleagues who died there.

I can never forget that, out of this great human tragedy, there was forged a great bond of friendship between the cities of Manchester and Munich.

I can never forget the wise words of the British Consul in Munich, Mr J. Somers-Cocks, who told me: 'I believe this terrible accident has done more for Anglo-German relations than any other single incident in my career with the Consular Service.'

I can never forget the joy and surprise on the faces of Professor Maurer, Professor Kessel, Dr Lechner and so many of the doctors and nurses who took care of me, when I went back to the Rechts der Isar Hospital with my wife and sons to show them I could walk again.

And, although I no longer report soccer every week, as I did for so many years, the links which Fate decreed I should have with Manchester United cannot be broken until I die. So, let us see, how this great club, born out of a war-time partnership between Matt Busby and Jimmy Murphy, survived the most savage blow ever dealt any football club in this country.

23 United Reborn

Three men, in my opinion, saved Manchester United from oblivion. They are: Jimmy Murphy, the loyal lieutenant of Matt Busby; Bobby Charlton, who was in such a dazed and shocked condition himself immediately after the accident that it seemed he might never play again; and Busby himself.

Murphy was perhaps the key figure. Only a strange twist of fate prevented him joining the United party on that trip. And when he came out to see the injured in Munich hospital, he found Matt close to death's door, and seven of the wonderful boys he had coached and trained dead.

In his shattered state Matt still found the courage to whisper to Murphy:

'Keep the flag flying, Jimmy, until I get back.'

And this extraordinary Welshman, with the Irish sounding name, did just that. In the first League match that United had to play after the crash, against Sheffield Wednesday, the club programme had to be printed with 11 vacant spaces for the United team. Murphy was forced to improvise. From Blackpool he bought little Ernie Taylor who, although short in stature, had the football brain to make him the general of the team.

From Aston Villa, Murphy bought a tough tackling wing half-back, Stan Crowther.

From then on, Murphy had to patch up the side as best as he could, with a mix of first teamers like Harry Gregg, Dennis Viollet, Bill Foulkes and Bobby Charlton; then he had to dig deep to bring on the very young players long before their time to serve United.

At first there were doubts whether the talented Charlton would ever play again. He seemed to be suffering from delayed shock, so Murphy packed him off to recoup with his own folk in Ashington. It worked.

Charlton became a key player as Murphy, the passionate Celt, breathed fire, fury, and pride back into this makeshift United team, to such an extent that, against all odds, they fought their way through to the 1958 Wembley Cup Final. In so doing, they fulfilled the promise that Busby had made a year earlier when he told his Babes, after losing the 1957 Cup Final to Aston Villa, that he expected them to come back to Wembley for the 1958 Cup Final.

Sadly, there was no happy ending to this fairy tale. It was sheer guts and crowd hysteria that had taken United to Wembley, but, once there, they couldn't match the experience of Bolton Wanderers led by Nat Lofthouse.

Nevertheless, Jimmy Murphy had worked the miracle United needed. How easy it would have been, once the first weeks of sympathy had subsided, to see United gradually slip down out of the First Division and become just another struggling League club.

Jimmy Murphy worked night and day to prevent that happening. By taking his makeshift Manchester United team to Wembley he gave the club back its pride. He forced the players and the supporters to realise Manchester United could become great again.

Matt Busby, tired and far from well, managed to leave his sick bed in Munich and come back to England to see that Cup Final. It was a brave gesture, although it was not long before Matt had to go back into hospital for further treatment, and his recovery took years rather than months. Yet always at his side was Jimmy Murphy, who preferred to be with his players than to court publicity.

Let no one doubt Jimmy Murphy's contribution to this club. In a sense he was born to be a backroom boy, at his best with the young players in the dressing room, rather than exchanging small talk in the Board Room. In his time, he had plenty of chances of moving up the ladder to become a fully fledged manager himself. He wasn't interested, not even when he was offered the managership of Liverpool, before Bill Shankly took it on.

Once he had signed for Manchester United to help Matt Busby build his dream club, Jimmy Murphy decided that would be his mission in life.

An emotional, warm-hearted man to those who know him,

fate decreed that Murphy would be the man to start the rebuilding of the club at a time when Busby was fighting for his life. He would not claim any credit because he is not that kind of man.

But once, when I was talking to him about his fears and his struggles to keep the flag flying, the mask slipped and I saw just how much agony he had gone through.

'It's a miracle you and Matt are here,' he said. 'After what you suffered . . . It was terrible.' Then Murphy stopped for a moment, and the tears came streaming down his face as he added: 'I suffered too. I said "cheerio" to Tommy Taylor, Duncan and all the lads in the gymnasium and told them I would see them back in the gymnasium on Friday . . . only when they came back to Old Trafford they were in their coffins . . .'

British sport would be richer if we had more people like Jimmy Murphy around. A loyal servant, a soccer expert in his own right, and yet content to be No 2 to a man he always rated as No 1 in the game.

When I asked Murphy what was the worst problem he had to face after Munich, he replied: 'The loss of Duncan Edwards. It was devastating for us and for England.'

When I asked Murphy to explain what he meant by that remark he replied: 'You sports writers use the word "great" when describing a soccer player far too often. Tom Finney was a great player, so was Alex James, so was John Charles, and so was Duncan Edwards. Great players occur perhaps once in a decade. My definition of a great player is one who not only has talent, but who motivates every other member of the team. When you have a truly great player you start with him, and then build the rest of the team around him. That's what made the loss of Duncan such a savage one. You could have played him anywhere and he would have done the job.'

I understood what Jimmy meant. United have so far not found another Duncan Edwards, nor for that matter has England. But eventually they had a very creditable substitute in Bobby Charlton.

At the time of the Munich crash Bobby Charlton was not even certain of his place in the United first team. He was then what would be called today a striker. He played upfield with Tommy

Taylor, waiting for the big man to head the ball back or lay it off to him. Then Thunderboots Charlton shot for goal.

After the accident they tried Bobby as an orthodox inside-forward, then at outside-left, where it was felt he would have the room to make the best use of his powerful shooting and his explosive bursts for goal. In theory it sounded all right, but when I saw Charlton at outside-left, he would make a surging run down the touchline, then hesitate as though wondering what to do next.

Eventually, after a lot of experimenting, Matt Busby played Charlton in the position in which football followers remember him best – as a deep-lying centre-forward, using his ability to hit long accurate passes to both wings, and occasionally coming through on his own to have a shot at goal. And it was in this position, in 1966 for England, and in 1968 for Manchester United, that Bobby Charlton had the greatest moments of his long and illustrious career.

It was hardly surprising, in view of his injuries, that it took a few years before Matt Busby recovered his health sufficiently to make his last big impact on the game he has served so well.

You could gauge the state of his recovery by the kind of players he either bought or produced from his youth teams. One must remember that Busby had three great sides at Old Trafford. The first he more or less inherited when he joined the club in 1945. Players such as Johnny Carey and Stan Pearson were already there; then Busby, with shrewd buys like Jimmy Delaney, the Scotsman many had thought was finished, gradually created what is generally recognised to be the most entertaining and classic football team in the immediate post-war era.

Using that side as his springboard Busby created his ideal club team by finding and developing the best young players he and his staff could discover . . . Thus were born the Busby Babes.

On his return to football, Busby found a changed situation. He had to scrap his former ideas and strengthen his team with shrewd moves in the transfer market. This had never been his style, but few could argue that he bought sensibly.

Among the players he bought were Albert Quixall from Sheffield Wednesday; David Herd (son of his former Manchester City team mate Alex Herd), from Arsenal; Pat Crerand from Glasgow Celtic, a classic, slow-moving wing half-back with great vision, who could change the entire pattern of a match with one accurate long pass. Then came Denis Law.

He was, as Busby once told me, the last ace in the pack. It was Busby who first told me about Law, when he was only a 15-year-old. We were coming back with Manchester United by coach from a Cup tie at Hartlepool in 1957, when Busby said to me: 'There is a kid playing at Huddersfield, who looks as though he is going to be as successful as Peter Doherty and Alex James . . . He's not the size of two pennyworth of copper but you can't keep him out of the game.'

'What's his name?' I asked.

'Denis Law,' Matt replied. 'Keep your eye on him.'

In fact Busby tried to persuade Andy Beattie, then manager at Huddersfield, as well as his right hand man Bill Shankly, to let Law come to Old Trafford for a £10,000 fee.

As the boy had never even played in League football at that time, you could argue United were taking a gamble, especially as it was known Law had needed an eye operation to correct his vision.

Beattie refused the offer, so Law made his way first in the Huddersfield team and was later transferred to Manchester City, then Torino. It was from the Italian club that Busby eventually got his man – for £110,000. As Matt said many, many time, 'Worth every penny. Once we got Denis I knew United were on the way back again as a great club.'

Busby and Murphy needed all their faith before that prophecy came true. In 1958, despite their savage losses at Munich, Manchester United finished ninth in the League. The following year they were runners-up to Wolves, although soccer experts realised they were in a false position. In 1960 they dropped to seventh, a position they held the following year. Then came the decline. In 1962 Manchester United finished 15th and it was obvious they were in danger of being relegated unless the team could be strengthened. One would have thought the arrival of Crerand and Law would have done the trick; in fact, in 1963 they had a desperate struggle to avoid relegation. Every week there were meetings to try and find what was going wrong, but both Busby and Murphy refused to panic. They insisted they had the right players to bring the club success.

And this is where I come into the story. In January 1963 I went to Coventry to cover a football match, and while there bought a postcard depicting the new Coventry Cathedral, because I knew Professor Frank Kessel in Munich was interested in it.

I sent the postcard to the Rechts der Isar Hospital and addressed it to Professor Frank Kessel, Chairman, Manchester United Supporters' Club (Munich Branch). For some reason I wrote 'Matt is strengthening your team . . . keep yourself free. They're going to win the Cup this year . . .' I posted it, and thought nothing more about it until April, when I received a letter from Professor Kessel in which he said he was feeling tired, but did not want to trouble Matt Busby, because he would have enough people scrounging for tickets. However, if I could get him a Cup Final ticket without too much trouble, he would love to come to see United at Wembley.

Frank Kessel got his ticket all right – courtesy of Matt Busby – and with it an invitation to Manchester United's Cup Final party at the Savoy.

This was the Cup Final in which Denis Law made Wembley his own personal stage, to give one of the greatest virtuoso performances even seen on that famous ground . . . and that, if I may say so, includes the 1953 Stanley Matthews Final.

I sat with Frank Kessel, and felt that some part of our debt had been paid when I saw his mounting excitement, as United beat Leicester City 3–1. Kessel, one of the finest brain surgeons in Europe, was like a schoolboy in his enthusiasm. 'Marvellous . . . marvellous . . . I am so happy to be here to see the final act after the tragedy in Munich,' he said.

I knew what he meant. He was still talking excitedly about the game as we travelled back by limousine to Mount Royal Hotel. He went upstairs to change for the banquet, and after what seemed an interminable time, he telephoned down for me to come to his room. I was shocked by what I saw. His nose was streaming with blood, but he was laughing. 'What a fine surgeon I am,' he said. 'In my joy and excitement at United's victory I have burst a blood vessel, and I haven't brought swabs to staunch the flow of blood. You must go, my dear Frank, to join Matt at the Savoy, and I will come on later.'

'I'm not going if you don't come with me,' I replied firmly.

'Don't spoil things for Matt and his team,' Frank said. 'You must go and present my respects. I will be able to come in an hour. I promise.'

So I went to the Savoy alone, found my place at the table I had been assigned and sat down to enjoy the meal and wait for Frank. As I did so, I noticed a rather nervous looking gentleman wandering from table to table, anxiously looking at the place names. Eventually he reached my table and confessed: 'I have been invited to the banquet by Mr Busby, but I can't find my place. What shall I do?'

I waved to a vacant seat next to me. 'There will be no one sitting here,' I said. 'Take this place.'

The stranger was profuse in his thanks, and eventually, after two glasses of wine, started to open up.

'It's very kind of you to let me sit here,' he said, 'because I've never been in a swell place like this before.'

'I can assure you, I don't come to the Savoy every night,' I replied.

'Well, sir,' he said. 'The fact is, my boy has signed for Manchester United, and he's been a little homesick. Mr Busby says he thinks my boy will be a star if he settles down in Manchester. I hope he proves Mr Busby right. It would be wonderful if he did become a famous player like Bobby Charlton.'

Without being unkind, I had heard similar stories from proud fathers before, and I was beginning to think the stranger was perhaps a little affected by the euphoria of the Cup success and the ever-flowing glasses of wine. Giving me his card, he rather plaintively added: 'That's my name, sir, if ever you can help my son with his career, I would be very grateful. Sometimes these young footballers listen to sports writers like you.'

Out of the corner of my eye I saw Frank Kessel approaching, so I put the card in my pocket and forgot all about it. I wanted Frank Kessel to enjoy every moment of that wonderful evening, and I am happy to say he did.

From that first day when he spoke to me in my hospital room I had had rapport with this wonderful man. Wherever I went in the world, I wrote to him or sent him postcards. I was happy for him yet a little saddened, when he wrote one day that he had had enough and that it was time for him to retire. So he left Munich and settled in Sweden.

I wrote to him from Christchurch in February 1974, whither I had gone to report the Commonwealth Games for the *Daily Mirror*. For once I did not get an immediate reply. Some weeks passed and then I received a letter from Sweden. It was from his widow, thanking me for the card and explaining that Frank had died peacefully a few weeks earlier.

Thus passed one of the biggest influences on my life, a man who had suffered much himself, but never showed it. A great surgeon who did not hide behind his diplomas, but a warm-hearted human being with many wide-ranging interests outside his dedicated service to medicine and the relief of suffering. A man I privately revered, who gave me hope when I needed it most. A man whose middle name was compassion.

I had tried to get him to come to Wembley in 1968 when Manchester United at last reached the final of the European Cup. He declined, saying that he wished them well, but he felt the match might be an anti-climax after seeing the Cup Final triumph five years earlier.

'Winning the English Cup was the match I wanted to see,' he wrote, 'because I knew that signified that the sad accident on the Munich airfield was now behind Matt and his players. The nightmare was over. Now they could only go forward to better things.'

It was a pity that Professor Kessel did not see the European Cup Final, firstly because he had an affinity with the city of Manchester, stemming from the friendliness he had found there when he escaped from Austria at the time of the Anschluss in 1938, to carry on his work as a neurosurgeon in Manchester Royal Hospital. Secondly, because he spoke English fluently, he had become so friendly with many of the Manchester United survivors that I humorously nicknamed him President of the Manchester United Supperters' Club in Munich. Certainly he took a very deep and abiding interest, not only in the progress of the survivors, but in the later successes of the team. Kessel had a sound knowledge and great interest in all sports, whereas Professor Maurer's life centred almost exclusively on his work and on his hospital.

Kessel would have been very moved at the reception Matt Busby and his team received at Wembley, when they met Benefica of Portugal. This was hardly fair on Benefica who played a sporting game, but the fact was, the entire crowd became Manchester United supporters for the night. They knew they were about to witness the last act in a great human drama. Eleven years previously Busby had risked his reputation by taking his young team into the European Cup. A year later he had had that great team decimated in an air crash. Britain's football fans had watched his long and painful path to recovery and the disappointments he had suffered on the way. In 1965, as League Champions, Manchester United had made their third attempt to win this elusive trophy, and looked like doing so; then those hopes were cruelly dashed in Belgrade, when the young genius, George Best, limped off the field with a cartilage injury which necessitated an operation. Now, three years later, most experts considered this to be United's best chance, especially when an incredible goal from Bill Foulkes, one of the Munich survivors, rallied United to win a match against their old rivals Real Madrid, which they were in danger of losing.

Foulkes in many ways epitomised the spirit of United. Although not a great or stylish player, nevertheless the former coal miner from St Helens proved to be a formidable competitor, whether playing at right-back or centre-half, the position in which he ended his career.

As the teams emerged from the dark tunnel on to the green Wembley pitch, you could tell by the tight lips and jutting jaw that Foulkes meant business. Charlton seemed lost in concentration. As usual, George Best seemed the least concerned player on view. Busby himself looked serious, although his face broke into a broad smile as 100,000 fans roared his name: 'BUSBY . . . BUSBY!' He knew. The crowd knew. This was the moment of truth.

High above the pitch in the Wembley Press Box someone asked me if I thought United would win.

'Win? Of course they'll win,' I replied, 'because they have GOT to win. If I know Bobby Charlton, he won't leave that pitch without the European Cup in his hands.'

Nevertheless, the tenseness that the United players felt was reflected in their play. They were trying to be too careful, too precise; and there was no fire and fury about their play. Not for the first time, I regretted there was no Duncan Edwards driving his team on. Charlton and Brian Kidd never stopped running, and it was this, and the non-stop encouragement of the crowd, which eventually brought United the goal they needed. At first in the Press Box we could hardly believe it, because Charlton – who like other great goal scorers, such as Jackie Milburn and Kenny Dalglish, was rarely seen to head the ball – had actually scored with a glancing header.

The Wembley crowd were willing United to win, but, one must be honest, they didn't dominate or control the game as everyone hoped, and it was hardly a surprise when Benefica equalised to take the game in to extra time.

It was heartbreaking watching Matt Busby and Jimmy Murphy moving among their players, urging them to even greater efforts in those extra 30 minutes. Surely Matt was not going to be robbed of the prize which had cost him, and the club, so much?

George Best gave the answer in the first few minutes of extra time. For most of the game, Best had seemed far below his formidable match-winning form, until this extraordinary moment when there seemed no possible danger to Benefica. Pat Crerand took a throw-in on the left side of the field, sending the ball to the left back Brennan. He rolled the ball back to the goalkeeper, Alex Stepney, who held the ball for a few seconds and then rolled it back to Brennan. The latter first essayed a kick upfield, then instead turned and played the ball back a second time to Stepney.

'Time-wasting,' I said to my neighbour. 'What's the good of passing back to the goalkeeper all the time? Besides Stepney is not kicking so accurately in this match.'

How wrong I was. I forgot to take George Best into my calculations. I have a ciné film of the incident, and you can see Best standing out on the left touchline until Stepney kicked the ball. The Irishman, with that uncanny anticipation possessed only by players of his genius, realised the Benefica centre-back wouldn't get it, so George sprinted in to the middle of the field, just in time to collect the ball as it brushed the head of the Benefica defender. Then he was off, the ball under perfect control, rounding a defender, drawing the goalkeeper, then cheekily taking the ball round him before pushing the ball in to the empty net.

Most players would have shot hard and hoped for the best. Not George Best; he had the confidence in his own ability to make absolutely sure he would score. There was no holding Manchester United after that. They had one hand on that European Cup and they weren't going to let it slip away a second time. Brian Kidd scored a third with a header, and Bobby Charlton capped probably the finest match he ever played at Wembley, by sweeping a centre from Kidd on the right wing into the net with stunning accuracy. It was all over. Tears and smiles and bear hugs for Busby and his team. The players wanted Matt to go up and receive the Cup, but he waved them away: 'It's your day . . . go on, Bobby . . . it's your day, son.'

Crowds in their thousands milled round the Russell Hotel in London that night. I was only one of many who never went to bed as the celebrations went on until dawn.

At first I was rather taken aback, on entering the dimly lit banqueting hall, by the sea of unidentifiable faces. Then a stranger grabbed the sleeve of my jacket and smiled:

'Do you remember me, Mr Taylor?'

I looked hard. Yes, I had seen the face before, but who he was I couldn't say. To make things easier, I smiled back at him and said:

'I know the face, old pal. But I have just forgotten the name.'

'I can't say I blame you,' said the stranger. 'We have met only once, and that was when United won the Cup in 1963. I'm the fellow you kindly let sit at your table. I told you then, I hoped my son had signed for Manchester United and I hoped he would make a name for himself. Didn't he play well tonight! There he is . . .'

I looked to where the stranger was pointing and saw George Best, a glass of champagne in his hand, chatting to a pretty girl. 'That's my son . . . George Best . . .'

Sometimes at these banquets, it is rather nice to slip away on your own to some quiet spot on the periphery of the milling throng. That's what I did on this occasion, standing by the door half hidden behind a curtain, ruminating on the past.

Ten years previously a number of people in that room had seen death at the end of the runway at Munich Airport. I was happy to see Johnny Berry far better than I had imagined he would be. Happy to see Bill Foulkes, and Matt and Jimmy Murphy savouring the joy of this night, as they were entitled to do. I was pleased to see the parents and relatives of the players who had been killed among those celebrating a great and historic victory.

One man who ought to have been there was missing . . . Bobby Charlton. I looked in vain and couldn't see him. Then his wife came through the door.

'Where is our Bob?' I asked. For a split second she looked embarrassed, and then whispered in my ear:

'It has all been a bit too much for Bobby. I think you would understand better than most people. He is just too tired physically and emotionally to face up to all this. He couldn't take it, with complete strangers coming up and slapping him on the back and telling him what a wonderful night it is . . . He's remembering the lads who can't be here tonight.'

I knew what Mrs Charlton meant. While the champagne flowed, and there was laughter and singing, Bobby Charlton was in his bed wiping away the tears, no doubt wishing, as those of us who are left wished, that Roger Byrne, Duncan Edwards, Tommy Taylor, Liam Whelan, Eddie Colman, David Pegg and Geoff Bent, could have been with us to share that happy ending to the Munich Story.

A Last Farewell to Sir Matt

The last time I saw Sir Matt Busby was an autumn night in 1993 when I sat next to him at Old Trafford watching Manchester United play the famous Hungarian side Honved in the European Cup.

Even in his 84th year Matt's face was a picture of expectancy, just as I remembered that first time when as a young reporter, I travelled into Europe with Manchester United.

As the teams came on to the pitch he tapped me on the knee. 'Just like old times, Frank,' he said. 'We are back where we belong, in Europe.'

We were sitting in the front row of the directors' box and I could not help but notice the group of Asian soccer fans in the row in front, nudging each other and turning to point at Busby. As the whistle blew for half-time they turned round, thrusting autograph books and pieces of paper at Matt. 'Please sign, Sir Busby,' they said.

Their leading spokesman explained. 'We are Manchester United supporters from Malaysia . . . This is my team and it is worth coming all this way to see them play because I've now met the greatest man in football . . . It is wonderful.'

Matt sat patiently signing his name. 'These are the people who count in soccer,' he said. 'If you don't keep them entertained and happy, where would the game be . . . ?'

A typical comment from Matt. That was always his style.

As I looked out over the pitch at Old Trafford, I thought of Matt fighting for his life in that oxygen tent next to my bed in the Rechts der Isar Hospital, I recalled yet again those whispered words to Jimmy Murphy: 'Keep the flag flying, Jimmy, until I get back.'

That was the start of the re-birth of Manchester United. But for the fighting spirit Matt displayed then, I doubt whether any of us at Old Trafford that night would have been watching European soccer. He saved the club and kept the flame of hope alive.

At a meal we had later that same evening, I asked Matt how he felt about the present United:

'Alex Ferguson is doing a great job,' he said, 'He is keeping faith with the United tradition by playing attractive football. In the years gone by I always said Real Madrid was the best team in Europe, and our team with Duncan Edwards, Roger Byrne, Eddie Colman and Tommy Taylor was the best young side in Europe, capable of eventually taking over the mantle from Real Madrid . . . The crash ended those hopes.

'I have high hopes of Alex's team. I think they can go all the way to win the European Cup. I hope they can achieve all we did and more . . . but I know in my heart no one can ever forget what those young boys did as the first English team to challenge Europe's best . . . They were UNFORGETTABLE.'

Sadly, a few months later Matt passed away. Thousands ignored the drenching rain, lining the streets of Manchester to pay their final respects to the Boss. They had not forgotten what he did for the club and the city or what the Busby Babes did to carry the flag of English football with honour and distinction around the world.